Contract Law in Brazil

Contract Law in Brazil

Lisiane Feiten Wingert Ody
Véra Maria Jacob de Fradera

This book was originally published as a monograph in the International Encyclopaedia of Laws/Contracts.

Founding Editor: Roger Blanpain
General Editor: Frank Hendrickx
Volume Editor: Jacques Herbots

Wolters Kluwer

Published by:
Kluwer Law International B.V.
PO Box 316
2400 AH Alphen aan den Rijn
The Netherlands
E-mail: international-sales@wolterskluwer.com
Website: lrus.wolterskluwer.com

Sold and distributed by:
Wolters Kluwer Legal & Regulatory U.S.
7201 McKinney Circle
Frederick, MD 21704
United States of America
Email: customer.service@wolterskluwer.com

ISBN 978-94-035-3310-0

e-Book: ISBN 978-94-035-3311-7
web-PDF: ISBN 978-94-035-3312-4

The Authors

Dr Véra Maria Jacob de Fradera PhD completed her Doctorate in Law at the University of Paris II (Pantheon Assas). During the doctoral course, she worked for two years as *lecturer* at the Comparative Institut of Paris II, IDC. She obtained her Master's in Private Law from the same university (Paris II). Specialization courses in German Law, Spanish Law and Community Law at the University of Paris complemented her European academic education. She also has a degree in Latin and Greek from the Pontifical Catholic University of Rio Grande do Sul.

She worked at UFRGS Law School from 1990 until her retirement in 2012. She was a guest professor at the Universities of Paraná (Brazil), Paris II, Rennes I, Strasbourg, Léon, Burgos, Buenos Aires, Venice and Trieste.

She is a member of the Society of Comparative Law, France, since 1989, and in 2001 she became a member of the International Academy of Comparative Law (IACL).

She published her doctoral thesis *Reflexões sobre a Contribuição do Direito Comparado para a elaboração do Direito Comunitário* (Thoughts on the Influence of the Comparative Law on the Formation and Elaboration of Community Law), written under the supervision of Mrs. Camille Jauffret-Spinosi. She is involved in collective works in Brazil, Argentina, Belgium, Canada, England, Germany, Vietnam, Mexico, Paraguay, France and the United States. She is also the author of numerous scholarly articles published in Brazil, Argentina, Belgium, France, and the United States and a member of the Scientific Committee of several legal periodicals.

The Authors

Dr Lisiane Feiten Wingert Ody PhD completed her Doctorate in Law at the Federal University of Rio Grande do Sul (UFRGS) in Brazil. During the doctoral course, she conducted research at Heidelberg University, Germany supervised by Dr Thomas Pfeiffer PhD, while sponsored by CAPES (Higher Education Personnel Improvement Coordination). She obtained her Master's in Private Law from UFRGS, also with a CAPES scholarship. Specialization courses in Environmental Law and Consumer Protection Law at UFRGS and in Civil Procedure at PUC-RS (Pontifical Catholic University of Rio Grande do Sul) complemented her academic education. As a student she took part in the DAAD (German Academic Exchange) programme *Winterkurs* at Albert-Ludwigs-Universität Freiburg, Germany.

She worked as a lecturer at UFRGS Law School from 2004 to 2005 and 2009 to 2011 and gave the introductory course on Brazilian Law at Heidelberg University in 2008.

Since having been chosen on the basis of a public tender in 2012, she has been Professor of Civil Law and Comparative Law at UFRGS. She is the author of the book *Einführung in das brasilianische Recht* (*Introduction to Brazilian Law*) published by C.H. Beck publishing house in Germany, and *Direito e Arte* (*Law and Art*) published by the Marcial Pons publishing house in Spain. Her main fields of work are comparative law and private law, especially civil law.

Since 2007 she has been a member of the association *Deutsch-Lusitanische Juristenvereinigung e.V. – DLJV* and runs legal study groups on comparative private law and copyright at UFRGS.

Table of Contents

The Authors 3

List of Abbreviations 13

Preface 15

General Introduction 17

§1. General Background: European Roots of Brazilian Private Law 17

§2. Brazil's Legal Family 24

§3. The Primacy of Statute in the Brazilian Judicial System 27

§4. Position of the Judiciary 28

§5. Distinction Between Public Law and Private Law 29

§6. Distinction Between Civil Law and Commercial Law 30

Introduction to the Law of Contracts 33

§1. Definition of Contract 33

§2. Historical Background of the Law of Contracts 33

§3. Classification of Contracts 35

I. Formation and Effects: Unilateral/Non-synallagmatic and Bilateral/Synallagmatic Contracts 35

II. Requirements of Form: Formal and Informal Contracts 36

III. Relationship of Dependency: Principal and Accessory Contracts 36

IV. Moment of the Formation: Consensual and Real Contracts 36

V. Time of Performance: Instantaneous and Continuous Performance 36

VI. Existence of the Reciprocal Benefits: Commutative and Aleatory Contracts 37

VII. Typical and Atypical Contracts 38

VIII. Civil and Commercial Contracts 38

IX. Transferability: Personal Service Contracts and Non-personal Service Contracts 39
X. Drafting: Adhesion Contracts 39
XI. Standard-Form Contracts 40

§4. CONTRACT AND TORTS 40
I. Burden of Proof (*ônus da prova*) 42
II. Differences Concerning the Capacity of the Tortfeasor 42
III. Graduation of the Fault 43

§5. CONTRACTS AND QUASI-CONTRACTS 44

§6. CONTRACTS AND LAW OF PROPERTY 44

§7. CONTRACTS AND TRUST 44

§8. GOOD FAITH (*BOA-FÉ*) AND FAIR DEALING 44

§9. STYLE OF DRAFTING 46

§10. SOURCES OF THE LAW OF CONTRACTS 48

Part I. General Principles of the Law of Contract 53

Chapter 1. Formation of a Contract 53

§1. AGREEMENT A *QUID PRO QUO* (RECIPROCITY) 53
I. Offer and Acceptance 53
II. Intent to Create Legal Relations 54
III. Offer and Acceptance in Adhesion Contracts 55
IV. Consideration 56
A. Gratuitous Promises 57
B. Natural Obligations 57
V. Modifications to the Contract 57

§2. FORMAL AND EVIDENTIAL REQUIREMENTS 59
I. Formal Requirements 59
II. Evidential Requirements: Proof 60
A. The Parol Evidence Rule 60
B. Role of the Notary 60
C. Burden of Proof: Distinction Between Obligation of Means and Obligation of Results 61

§3. LIABILITY AND NEGOTIATIONS 62
I. Pre-contractual Liability 62
A. Forms of Pre-contractual Relationships Generally Admitted in Legal Transactions 63

B. Reactions to Faulty Behaviour in the Pre-contractual Phase: Brazilian Solutions 64
II. Ihering's Discovery: The Notion of *Culpa in Contrahendo* 65
III. Conclusion 66

Chapter 2. Conditions of Substantive Validity 67

§1. Capacity of the Parties 67

§2. Defects of Consent 69
I. Error (Distinction from Value; Distinction from Motive)/ Misrepresentation and Deceit 69
II. Improper Pressure 71
III. Gross Disparity 72

§3. Other Conditions of Validity 74
I. Existing and Licit Object 74
II. Determined or Determinable, Possible and Licit Object or a Lack of Substantive Validity 75
III. Initial Impossibility 76

§4. The Consequences of a Defect of Consent or a Lack of Substantive Validity 76
I. Avoidance of the Contract: Nullity 76
II. Retroactive Effect of Avoidance or Nullity 77
III. Relative Nullity or Possibility of Annulment of the Transaction 77
IV. Damages 78

Chapter 3. Contents of a Contract 79

§1. Different Clauses 79
I. Ascertaining Express Terms 79
II. Implied Terms 80
III. Standard Terms and Exemption Clauses 80
IV. Penalty Clauses 81
V. Arbitration Clauses 82

§2. Interpretation 84

§3. Conditional Contracts 85

Chapter 4. Privity of Contract 87

§1. Rule of Privity of Contract 87
I. Third Parties and the Contract 87

II. Contract for the Benefit of a Third Party (*contratos em favor de terceiros*) 88

§2. Transfer of Contractual Rights 88

§3. Special Case: Subcontracts 88

§4. *Actio Pauliana* 88

Chapter 5. Termination of Contract 90

§1. Performance and Breach 90

§2. Impossibility, Frustration and Hardship: The Unforeseen 90

§3. Discharge by Agreement 90

Chapter 6. Remedies 91

§1. General Provisions 91

§2. Specific Performance and Injunctions: *Astreintes* 91

§3. Termination 93

§4. *Exceptio Non Adimpleti Contracts* 95

§5. Faulty Behaviour of the Debtor 96

§6. Limitation of Actions 99

§7. Damages and Exemption Clauses 100

§8. Restitution 101

Part II. Specific Contracts 105

Chapter 1. Agency 105

§1. Introduction 105

§2. Agency and Distribution Agreements 105
I. Definition of the Agency and Distribution Agreement 106
II. Characteristics of Agency and Distribution Agreements 106
III. Difference Between Agency and Distribution 107

Chapter 2. Rental Agreements 108

§1. Introduction 108

§2. Characteristics of Rental Agreements 108
I. Classification 108
II. Legal Nature 108
III. Parties 109
IV. Rent 109
V. Obligations of the Lessor and the Lessee 109
VI. Building Rentals 109

§3. Conclusion 110

Chapter 3. Gambling and Wagering 111

§1. Introduction 111

§2. Characteristics of Gambling and Wagering Contracts 111

§3. Types of Gambles 111

Chapter 4. Sale of Goods 113

§1. Introduction 113

§2. Essential Elements of the Sale of Goods 114

§3. Rights and Duties of the Parties in the Sale of Goods 115

§4. Secondary or Natural Elements of the Purchase and Sale Agreement 116

§5. Basic and Essential Obligations in Certain Types of Sale 116

§6. Expenses in the Sale of Goods 117

Chapter 5. Works Contracts 118

§1. Introduction 118

§2. Parties to Works Contracts 118

§3. Observations about the Similarities Between Works, Purchase and Sale and Employment Contracts 118

§4. Characteristic Features of Works Contracts 119

§5. Types of Works Contracts 119
I. Works Contract *of Labour* 119
II. Works Contract 120
III. Works Contracts for a Fixed Price 120

§6. Works Contract Risks 120

§7. Liability for the Solidity of the Works 120

§8. Conclusion 121

Chapter 6. Leasing 122

§1. Introduction 122

§2. Types of Leasing 123

Chapter 7. Settlements 125

§1. Settlement Form 125
I. Settlement Requirement 125
II. Settlement Types 125
III. Nullity of the Settlement 126
IV. Voidability of the Settlement 126

§2. Interpretation of Legal Settlement and Relevant Distinctions 126
I. Settlement Scope 126
II. Settlement and Eviction 127
III. Settlement and Criminal Offence 127

Chapter 8. Suretyship 128

§1. Introduction 128

§2. Elements of Suretyship Contract 128

§3. Conclusion 129

Chapter 9. Pledge (*Pignus*) 130

§1. Introduction 130

§2. Configuration of the Pledge Contract under the Brazilian Civil Code 131

§3. Rights and Obligations of the Secured Creditor 131

§4. Rights of the Debtor 132

§5. Termination of the Pledge 132

§6. Types of Pledges 133

Chapter 10. Loans 135

§1. Introduction 135

§2. Elements of the Loan for Use 135

§3. Duties of the Parties in the Loan for Use 136
I. Duties of the Loanee 136
II. Duties of the Loaner or Lender 136
III. Termination 137

§4. Elements of the Loan for Consumption 137
I. Definition 137
II. Characteristics 137

Chapter 11. Contracts with the Government and Other Public Administrations 139

§1. Characteristics 139

§2. Types of Administrative Contracts 142

Chapter 12. Partnership Agreements 144

Selected Bibliography 147

Index 155

List of Abbreviations

Art.	Artigo (Article)
BGB	Bürgerliches Gesetzbuch (German Civil Code)
CC	Código Civil Brasileiro (Brazilian Civil Code)
CCom	Código Comercial (Commercial Code)
CDC	Código de Defesa do Consumidor (Consumer Protection Code)
CF	Constituição Federal (Federal Constitution)
CLT	Consolidação das Leis do Trabalho (Consolidated Labour Law)
CNJ	Conselho Nacional de Justiça (National Justice Council)
EC	emenda constitucional (constitutional amendment)
ECA	Estatuto da Criança e do Adolescente (Child and Adolescent Statute)
LINDB	Lei de Introdução às Normas de Direito Brasileiro (Law of Introduction to the Rules of Brazilian Law)
MERCOSUL	Mercado Comum do Sul (Southern Common Market)
PEC	Proposta de Emenda Constitucional (Constitutional Amendment Bill)
PGR	Procurador Geral da República (Attorney General of the Republic)
REsp	Recurso Especial (Special Appeal)
S.A.	Sociedade Anônima (Limited Liability Company)
STF	Supremo Tribunal Federal (Federal Supreme Court)
STJ	Superior Tribunal de Justiça (High Court)

Súmula	súm. (Precedent)
TJ	Tribunal de Justiça (Court of Justice)

Preface

This monograph is included in the *International Encyclopaedia of Laws* (a collection published by Kluwer) and, in this context, is intended to introduce Brazilian contractual law to foreign students and law professionals.

To begin with, the general introduction provides some information on the background of Brazil and its legal system. The next part presents Brazilian contract law: first, by defining the term 'contract', its classifications and its relations with other branches of private law, such as tort law, quasi-contract and property law; second, it sets out the rules regarding contract formation, the conditions of substantive validity, the contents of a contract, the privity of contract, the termination of contract and remedies for breach of contract.

Afterwards, there is an analysis of selected contractual types such as agency, rental agreements, gaming and wagering, sale of goods, leasing, settlements, suretyship, pledge, loans, contracts with the government and other public bodies and partnership agreements.

The legal terms in Portuguese are presented in parentheses next to the equivalent English terms for clarification purposes. Any possible imperfection in the translation, due to absence of an exactly corresponding term, is clarified in a footnote.

The footnotes also contain bibliographical references in Portuguese to facilitate the search for local publications. It should be noted, however, that since the introduction of the famous 'Law of Good Reason' (Pt. *Lei da Boa Razão*),[1] Brazilian law has maintained the tradition of using references from foreign literature. This is because the Brazilian legal system is replete with legal transplants, hence arguments based on supposed authority are still widely used.

1. Law of Good Reason (Law of 18 Aug. 1769) which provided that it 'would be better to look for solutions in the legislation of civilized nations'.

Preface

General Introduction

§1. General Background: European Roots of Brazilian Private Law

1. Brazil – officially the Federative Republic of Brazil – is the largest country in both South America and Latin America. Globally, it is the fifth-largest country by area (8,515,767,049 km^2) and by population (more than 200 million inhabitants).

2. It is the largest Portuguese-speaking nation in the world and the only one in the Americas. Brazil is considered a multicultural nation since it was primarily formed by immigrants.

3. Brazil faces the Atlantic Ocean along 7,491 km of coastline and shares borders with every South American country except Chile and Ecuador – especifically Venezuela, Guyana, Suriname, and the French overseas department of French Guiana to the north; Colombia to the northwest; Bolivia and Peru to the west; Argentina and Paraguay to the southwest; and Uruguay to the south. The Brazilian territory also encompasses a number of archipelagos, such as the Rocas Atoll, Saint Peter and Paul Rocks, Fernando de Noronha (the only inhabited archipelago) and Trindade and Martim Vaz.

4. It is a federative presidential republic composed of the Federal District, 26 states and 5,570 municipalities.

5. During an expedition lead by *Pedro Álvares Cabral* in 1500, the Portuguese discovered the territory which is today known as Brazil.

6. Before *Pedro Álvares Cabral* discovered the coast of Brazil for the Portuguese crown on 22 April 1500,[2] large parts of Brazil's current territory were home to indigenous people. In 1534, the Portuguese King *Dom João III* (*King John III*) introduced a system of fifteen hereditary captaincies (*capitanias*).[3] Salvador da Bahia was the first capital city. Initially, the colony mainly exported sugar cane and Brazilwood (*Paubrasil*) which gave the country its name. When gold was discovered around Rio de Janeiro, the city became very prosperous and was declared the new capital city.

2. According to the Treaty of Tordesillas, signed on 7 Jun. 1494, the Portuguese crown instead of the Spanish crown owned the recently discovered land.
3. Schmidt, Zivilrechtskodifikation in Brasilien, pp. 13–16.

7. In colonial times, the Brazilian and Portuguese legal systems evolved in parallel. The Ordinations of the Portuguese Kings *Dom Afonso V* (*Ordenações Afonsinas*) in 1447, *Dom Manuel I* (*Ordenações Manuelinas*) in 1521, and *Dom Filipe II* (*Philip II – Ordenações Filipinas*) in 1603 are attributed central importance.[4] They were collections of codified Portuguese laws but lost their significance with increasing numbers of supplementary statutes.[5] In 1769, the *Lei da Boa Razão* (Law of Good Sense) which was influenced by the *Marquis of Pombal* was passed to fill the legislative gaps in the Ordinations.[6]

8. Therefore, Brazil's judicial system,[7] like those of all the other Latin American countries, belongs to the Romano-Germanic legal family which was developed in the twelfth century by universities in continental Europe under the strong influence of the Roman and Canonical system. In the nineteenth century, movements for independence arose in South America. Most of the countries fighting for their independence adopted republics as their form of government, with Brazil being the only exception, choosing monarchy under the Emperor Prince *Pedro 1 of Bragança*, the heir of *King John VI* of Portugal.

9. Expecting an imminent invasion by *Napoleon Bonaparte*'s troops in 1807, the Portuguese royal family fled from Lisbon to Rio de Janeiro, the future capital of the Portuguese empire.[8] In the presence of the Portuguese King, Rio de Janeiro and the whole colony enjoyed a considerable economic and cultural boom.[9] At the Congress of Vienna in 1815, the 'United Kingdom of Portugal, Brazil and the Algarves' was formed. In 1821, King *Dom João VI* (*John VI*)[10] returned to Lisbon, while his son *Pedro* remained in Brazil and declared the country's independence on 7 September 1822. He had crowned himself the Emperor of Brazil on 1 December 1822

4. European law was imposed on Brazil by the Ordinances [Ordenações] during the Portuguese colonization in the sixteenth and seventeenth centuries. The Ordinances were a set of rules inspired by the Roman, Canonical, Visigothic and Arab system. The Portuguese Emperor Charles V ruled Portugal and Spain making them both subject to the Ordinances.

   During the colonial period, throughout the sixteenth, seventeenth and eighteenth and early nineteenth centuries, these Ordinances underwent an interesting evolution as local judges and courts both in the Portuguese colony and in the rest of the continent applied and interpreted them. For details on the Ordinations, *see* Rathenau, Einführung in das portugiesische Recht, 2013, §2 paras 7–9, and Almeida Costa, História do Direito Português, 5th edition 2012, pp. 273 f.
5. Schmidt, Zivilrechtskodifikation in Brasilien, pp. 7 f.
6. Schmidt, Zivilrechtskodifikation in Brasilien, p. 9.
7. For further information about Brazilian legal system, *see*: Feiten Wingert Ody, Lisiane. *Einführung in das brasilianische Recht*. München: C.H. Beck, 2016.
8. For developments in Portugal, *see* Rathenau, Einführung in das portugiesische Recht, 2013, § 2 paras 11 f.
9. Schmidt, Zivilrechtskodifikation in Brasilien, pp. 16 f.
10. After his mother *Dona Maria I* was incapacitated in 1792, *João VI* initially assumed the reins of government as prince regent. Following *Maria's* death on 16 Mar. 1816, he became the head of the United Kingdom of Portugal, Brazil and the Algarves. His coronation took place on 2 Feb. 1818.

(*Pedro I do Brasil, Peter I of Brazil*). Due to political turmoil in Portugal,[11] he abdicated on 7 April 1832, returned to his country of birth and left the throne to his son *Pedro*, who was five years old at the time.

10. Meanwhile, other South-American nations declared themselves republics and started to elaborate legal codes for their people. The *Code Napoléon* served as a model because it represented the consolidation of the revolutionary ideas from 1789, inscribed in the Declaration of the Rights of Man and of the Citizen. In South America, only two countries did not follow the *Code Napoléon.* Besides Chile, Brazil – a sovereign monarchy – passed an independent code preserving many of the ancient Ordinances without, however, seeking inspiration in models considered modern at the time.

11. The first Brazilian constitution of 28 March 1824 stipulated the timely development of civil and criminal codes. In 1830, a modern criminal code entered into force, followed by a code of criminal procedure two years later.

12. *Dom Pedro II* (*Peter II*) was formally declared of age on 23 July 1840 and was crowned emperor the following year. During his reign until 15 November 1889, first coffee and later, in the 1870s, rubber was among the main export goods promoting the country's economic upturn.

13. Regardless of the constitutional prevision to create a civil code, a commercial code was first passed in March 1850 comprising three parts with 913 articles.[12] Lacking a civil code, the Commercial Code addressed several issues of general law of obligations. The regulations of the *Ordenações Filipinas* continued to apply as subsidiary rules. The 1850 Commercial Code's provisions on maritime trade remain valid until today.

14. The 'Golden Law' (*Lei Áurea*)[13] abolished slavery on 13 May 1888 leaving the Emperor without any support from the upper class whose wealth was mainly due to slave-based production of coffee and rubber. Many considered *Dom Pedro II* merely a representative of the former colonial empire of Portugal. Growing nationalist sentiment peaked when *Manuel Deodoro da Fonseca* proclaimed the Republic on 15 November 1889.[14] Initially, he was the head of a provisional government that passed Brazil's first republican constitution on 24 February 1891. It was strongly influenced by the US Constitution stipulating federalism. This constitution marked the era of the 'Old Republic' (*República Velha*) until 1930. *Manuel Deodoro da Fonseca* became Brazil's first directly elected president. The most populous and

11. In spite of an internal agreement, *Dom Pedro*'s younger brother *Miguel* was crowned to be king of Portugal causing a war referred to as the 'War of the Two Brothers' or the 'Miguelite War' (1832–1834), from which *Dom Pedro I* emerged victorious.
12. Schmidt, Zivilrechtskodifikation in Brasilien, pp. 21 ff.; Jaeger Jr., Das neue brasilianische Bürgerliche Gesetzbuch und das Unternehmensrecht, in: Jayme/Schindler (Hrsg.), Portugiesisch – Weltsprache des Rechts, 2004, pp. 217, 219.
13. Law n° 3.353 of 13 May 1888.
14. *Dom Pedro II* went into exile in France.

wealthiest states São Paulo and Minas Gerais had a particularly strong impact on the country's political development.[15] A small upper class evolved and accumulated wealth by exporting agricultural products, eventually resulting in the oligarchic rule.[16]

15. During the Old Republic, the first Brazilian Civil Code (CC/1916) entered into force on 1 January 1917. The groundwork for this code was laid by *Augusto Teixeira de Freitas* (1816–1883), who had already submitted a collection of all the valid civil laws (*Consolidação das Leis Civis*) existing in 1855 and a comprehensive subsequent draft code (*esboço*) in 1865.[17] *Clóvis Beviláqua* (1859–1944) originally drafted the code in 1899 which was profoundly influenced by late nineteenth century liberalism and individualism.[18] During the sixteen-year legislative process, the draft's language was revised primarily.

16. At that time, Brazil was a non-industrialized, agriculture-based country exporting coffee, sugar, cocoa, and other goods to the main European markets, which guaranteed the stability of the national currency. Industrialization began slowly after the end of the Second World War with most industries being concentrated in the state of São Paulo. As a consequence, the first social changes occurred in this period: Brazilian women, who were previously limited to domestic affairs, started working as employees in numerous factories.[19]

---

15. São Paulo's key role at the time originated in the production of coffee, while Minas Gerais prospered thanks to its dairy sector. This period is referred to as 'coffee and milk politics' (*política do café com leite*).
16. Since women and illiterate people had no voting rights, only about 5% of the population was eligible to vote, providing the framework for this development. Costa, Das politische System Brasiliens, in: Stüwe/Rinke (Hrsg.), Die politischen Systeme in Nord- und Lateinamerika, 2008, pp. 114, 115.
17. The government did not approve his draft Civil Code from 1868 due to the innovations it contained. For example, the Introductory Act to the Civil Code foresaw the application of the concept of domicile for international contracts, when, at that time, the majority of countries used the concept of nationality. Other innovative aspects in Freitas' draft were the unification of civil and commercial obligations and the granting of more freedom to married women. Despite all the progress, Freitas' draft lacked some important issues, such as a regulation for farmers' juridical relations. Schmidt, Zivilrechtskodifikation in Brasilien, pp. 26–41.
18. The Code showed particular characteristics such as the presence of Visigothic traditions in the Law of Successions and a prevailing influence of Canonical Law, particularly in Family Law, which was marked by the lack of equality between husband and wife as well as between children regarding legitimacy. The Law of Obligations and Law of Contracts were subject to Roman influence and thus resembled the German law of pandect from 1916 and, consequently, the BGB from 1900. The Code kept the substantial division between a General Part [Parte Geral] and a Special Part [Parte Especial]. At the time, political and economic liberalism predominated, making the private law system immune to interference from public law, following the maxim '*laisser faire, laisser passer*'. In addition, juridical individualism impacted Contractual Law, as the notion of contract prevailed over the idea of perfect equality and balance between the parties. Another contractual principle was the *caveat emptor*, which was a consequence of the juridical liberalism. For more details, *see*: Schmidt, Zivilrechtskodifikation in Brasilien, pp. 51–53.
19. For further information on this period of Brazilian political and legal development *see*: Legal Culture and Legal Transplants, *La Culture Juridique et l'Acculturation du Droit*, International Academy of Comparative Law, Universidad Autónoma de Mexico, Mexico, 2101, Editor Jorge A. Sanchez Cordero. Rapport National Brésilien par Vera Jacob de Fradera, Vol. I. p. 195.

17. *Getúlio Vargas* (1883–1954) marked the end of the Old Republic in 1930. Brazil's agriculture-oriented economy struggled during the Great Depression because of collapsing coffee prices. Assisted by the military, *Vargas* seized power on 3 November 1930. After a period of upheavals involving conflicts with the military, elections for a constitutional assembly were held on 3 May 1933. *Vargas* was elected president and proclaimed the *Estado Novo* ('New State') on 10 November 1937, which was a centralized dictatorship.

18. During the *Estado Novo*, a comprehensive Labour Code (*Consolidação das Leis do Trabalho,CLT*) was passed on 1 May 1943[20] providing individual and collective labour laws as well as regulations on labour proceedings.

19. In October 1945, the military removed *Vargas*. The new and democratic constitution of 18 September 1946 laid the foundations for the *República Nova* (first New Republic). The most famous president of this era was *Juscelino Kubitschek* (12 September 1902–22 August 1976) who was elected in 1955. During his administration, the architect *Oscar Niemeyer* built the new capital Brasília. The planned city was inaugurated on 21 April 1960.

20. In the early 1960s, the Brazilian economy struggled with high inflation rates and economic stagnation. Little by little, the State started to interfere in people's private sphere, opposing the 1916 Code's provisions. New laws were passed modifying the Civil Code absorbing some of the social achievements particularly for Brazilian women. The Married Woman Statute (*Estatuto da Mulher Casada*, Law n. 4.121 of 1962) was created.[21]

21. Counting on the support of the governors of the states Rio de Janeiro, Minas Gerais and São Paulo, the military carried out a coup on 31 March 1964. The presidents during the military regime were generals.

22. On 15 March 1967, a new constitution entered into force strengthening the military's rule. At the expense of the legislative branch, the executive branch gained extensive competences, e.g., the exclusive competence to regulate financial and security issues. The death penalty was introduced for crimes against national security. Moreover, the regime used Institutional Acts (*Atos Institucionais*) to override the constitution. For example, they were used to suspend direct presidential elections, cancel the mandates of members of the opposition, and dissolve political parties.[22] Institutional Act no. 5 of 13 December 1967[23] enabled the president to dissolve the National Assembly and other legislative bodies, which were only able

20. Decree-law nº 5.452 of 1 May 1943.
21. Only in 1977 the country adopted divorce through law nº 6.515.
22. Schmidt, Zivilrechtskodifikation in Brasilien, p. 67. Only two parties were allowed, namely *Aliança Renovadora Nacional* and *Movimento Democrático Brasileiro*.
23. Institutional Act no. 5 (*Ato Institucional nº 5*) suspended Habeas Corpus guarantees for certain crimes and determined the president's regulatory powers such as declaring the state of emergency, carrying out a federal invention without any constitutional restrictions, suspending political rights and limiting public or individual rights, permanently withdrawing the right to hold any elected office,

to hold meetings if the president summoned them. Furthermore, the judicial review of custodial measures (Habeas Corpus) and even reviews of Institutional Acts were restricted to a greater extent. A revised version of the 1967 Constitution was republished on 17 October 1969, to guarantee the superiority of Institutional Acts.

23. During the military regime, the presidents *Ernesto Geisel* and *João Baptista de Oliveira Figueiredo* advocated a more open military regime and democratic structures. Finally, the 1984 presidential election won by *Tancredo Neves* – not a general himself[24] – marked the beginning of the second New Republic (*Nova República*).[25] The Democratic Federal Constitution (*Constituição da República Federativa do Brasil*) of 5 October 1988[26] is still valid today; comprises a comprehensive catalogue of fundamental rights; stipulates a bicameral legislature with a parliament and a senate; and guarantees judicial independence.

24. This constitution was a major step forward from a political point of view not only since it restored the country's democracy but also because it updated the three fundamental bases of private law, which are family, property and contract. In family law, the constitutional legislator recognized the juridical effects of the *stable union* (*união estável*), granting legal protection to an informal union between man and woman. The 1934 Constitution in its Article 113 § 17 had already recognized the social purpose of property (*função social da propriedade)*, which was inspired by the German Weimar Constitution from 1919. The other Brazilian constitutions after 1934 followed the same principle, but the 1988 Constitution enlarged its scope: it reduced the period of time required for the appropriation of rural land to five years. For effective appropriation, the interested person needed to establish his or her home in the respective area and had to carry out a productive activity on it.

25. On 11 September 1990, a comprehensive Consumer Protection Code[27] entered into force. This Code was successful particularly because it revolutionized the way contracts were seen, calling attention to certain principles on the contractual relation, such as good faith[28] (*boa-fé objetiva*), loyalty and reliability, which were presupposed in the previous Civil Code and are now explicitly expressed in

---

and temporary ceasing the activities of the National Congress (*Congresso Nacional*), legislative parliaments (*Assembléias Legislativas*) and town councils (*Câmaras de Vereadores*). Article 5 excluded compliant acts and resulting Complementary Acts (*Atos Complementares*) from judicial review (*apreciação judicial*).

24. On health grounds, *Tancredo Neves* was unable to take office. *José Sarney* became president on 15 Mar. 1985.
25. The Portuguese language allows a distinction between the first New Republic (*República Nova*) and the second New Republic (*Nova República*) by positioning the adjective. English, however, requires ordinal numbers.
26. The Constitution was known as the 'Citizen Constitution' [*constituição cidadã].* Since the federal constitution took effect twenty-eight years ago, ninety amendments (*Emenda Constitucional, EC*) have been made to various parts of the constitution.
27. Lei nº 8.078/1990.
28. In its objective sense, that is, by imposing a standard of fair dealing on the obligatory relationship, based on standards that require the parties act cooperatively and are loyal to each other. It contrasts with the subjective sense, which refers to the individual subjective perception, of believing to be honest, which is referred to in Portuguese as subjective good faith.

the legal text. Another important aspect was the openness of Brazil's juridical ordinance to a European juridical model (provided by the European Community instead of a specific country) exemplified by the Consumer Protection Code which was inspired by the European Community Directive on Liability for Defective Products of 1985. Also regarding contracts, it is necessary to refer to the relevant role of the Brazilian doctrine, shaped particularly by the writings of three great jurists: *Pontes de Miranda,*[29] *Orlando Gomes*[30] and *Clóvis do Couto e Silva.*[31] The former introduced a cooperative notion of contracts to Brazilian Law, as an example of the Germanic system of contracts resulting from the vocation of Germanic peoples to exchange goods.

26. On 7 July 1994, after years of extremely high inflation, President *Itamar Franco* introduced a new currency the '*Real*' as part of a set of economic measures (*Plano Real*). Supporting these modifications and stabilizing the economy, *Fernando Henrique Cardoso*, the minister of finance of the social democratic party, became president of the Republic for two terms.

27. A fundamentally revised Civil Code (CC/2002) came into force on 11 January 2003.[32] In 1969, *Miguel Reale* (1910–2006) had already been employed to develop a reform proposal which he and six other lawyers concluded in 1975.[33] The Chamber of Deputies only passed the draft in 1984; political changes in the second half of the 1980s additionally delayed the negotiations in the Senate. Only in 1995, a Senate committee was set up to resume the work on the civil code. After remitting the proposal to the Chamber of Deputies in December 1997, it was passed by both legislative bodies in December 2001. A key characteristic of the CC/2002 is the fact that it unites civil and commercial law.

28. *Luis Inácio Lula da Silva* of the Workers' Party *PT* (*Partido dos Trabalhadores*) assumed the presidency on 1 January 2003. After him, *Dilma Rousseff* from the same party was elected. Following re-election in 2014, the *Rousseff* government and the President herself experienced a severe political crisis fuelled by economic and social problems. In April 2016, impeachment proceedings were opened against the President. Consequently, the Vice President *Michel Temer*, from the largest Brazilian party PMDB (*Partido do Movimento Democrático Brasileiro*) assumed the presidency and ruled the country until the elections of 2018. His party had been part of every government since the end of the dictatorship in 1985.

29. On 1 January 2019 *Jair Bolsonaro* assumed the presidency of the country.

29. Tratado de Direito Privado, 60 volumes. Rio de Janeiro: Borsoi, 1972.
30. Introdução ao Direito Civil, Editora Forense, Rio de Janeiro, 9th edition, 1987; Contratos, Editora Forense, Rio de Janeiro, 12th edition; Obrigações, Rio de Janeiro, Forense, 1960.
31. A obrigação como Processo, Editor José Bushastky, São Paulo, 1976.
32. Lei nº 10.406/2002.
33. Schmidt, Zivilrechtskodifikation in Brasilien, pp. 67–70 (Reale) and § 7 (Civil Code).

§2. BRAZIL'S LEGAL FAMILY

30. Being a former Portuguese colony, Brazilian law belongs to the civil law family.

31. When *Napoleon's* troops were marching on Portugal and the Portuguese King *Dom João VI* (*John VI of Portugal*) fled to colonial Brazil in the early nineteenth century, Portuguese law still applied to Brazil. One year after Brazil's independence in 1822, the first Emperor of Brazil, *Dom Pedro I* (*Peter I of Brazil*), passed a law stipulating that all Portuguese laws remained valid unless they were replaced by Brazilian laws.[34] The 1824 Constitution stated that Brazilian civil and criminal codes were to be created as soon as possible.[35] The criminal code was drafted and published in 1830. However, for the time being no civil code was developed. In the 1840s, Brazilian lawyers saw the urgent need to reform the existing and rather chaotic civil legislation. Five years after the new commercial code came into force in 1850,[36] *Augusto Teixeira de Freitas*, a famous lawyer from Rio de Janeiro, was assigned to develop a civil code.[37] He systematically collected all civil laws that were valid in Brazil between 1822 and 1857, and published them in 1858 with the title '*Consolidação das Leis Civis*'.[38] In the same year, the Ministry of Justice tasked him with a second step: developing a civil code.[39] Initially, he only wanted to draw up an '*Esbôço*' (draft), in order to give other lawyers the chance to offer criticism.[40]

32. His draft was a very sophisticated systematic approach to the subject matter providing a wide range of solutions. Thus, the '*Esbôço*' is considered one of the most impressive civil law works of the nineteenth century and was widely acclaimed by lawyers in Latin America and Europe.[41] When he was almost concluding the work on the *esboço* and its 4,908 articles, *Teixeira de Freitas* changed his original plan: instead of creating a new civil code, he decided to combine civil

34. Moreira Alves, A parte geral do Projeto de Código Civil Brasileiro: subsídios históricos para o novo Código Civil Brasileiro, 2003, pp. 3 ff.
35. Article 179 of the 1824 Constitution states: '*A inviolabilidade dos Direitos Civis, e Politicos dos Cidadãos Brazileiros, que tem por base a liberdade, a segurança individual, e a propriedade, é garantida pela Constituição do Imperio, pela maneira seguinte. (...) XVIII. Organizar-se-ha quanto antes um Código Civil, e Criminal, fundado nas solidas bases da Justiça, e Equidade*' in: Nogueira, Octaciano. Constituições Brasileiras: 1824. Brasília: Senado Federal e MCT, Centro de Estudos Estratégicos, 2001.
36. Moreira Alves, A parte geral do Projeto de Código Civil Brasileiro: subsídios históricos para o novo Código Civil Brasileiro, 2003, pp. 3 ff.
37. For the life and work of *Teixeira de Freitas, see*: Schipani, Augusto Teixeira de Freitas e il Diritto Latinoamericano: Atas do Congresso Internacional do centenário de Augusto Teixeira de Freitas, 1988, in particular the essays by Amaral Neto, Villela, Rescigno, Reale, Alves, and Luig.
38. Teixeira de Freitas, Consolidação das Leis Civis, 2003.
39. Moreira Alves, A parte geral do Projeto de Código Civil Brasileiro: subsídios históricos para o novo Código Civil Brasileiro, 2003, pp. 3 ff.
40. Teixeira de Freitas, Código Civil: Esboço, 1861, Preface.
41. Jacob de Fradera, La partie générale du Code Civil, in: Wald/Jauffret-Spinosi (Hrsg.), Le droit brésilien d'hier, d'aujourd'hui et de demain, 2005.

and commercial law in one code. However, his plan did not meet with the approval of the authorities and he was dismissed in 1872 before he was able to finish his work.

33. The task of drawing up a civil code was passed on to Senator *Nabuco de Araujo*, who died six years later unable to fulfil it,[42] and so a commission was set up to carry on the work. However, on 15 November 1889, Brazil abolished the monarchy and proclaimed the Republic, during which the contract with the commission was cancelled. In the new Republic, *Coelho Rodrigues*, a lawyer, was employed to develop a civil code. Having studied and worked in Switzerland, his proposal was strongly inspired by Swiss law and the Civil Code of the canton of Zurich. Regrettably, his work was not accepted.[43]

34. Consequently, *Clóvis Beviláqua* was fortunate enough to be charged with the task of drawing up a civil code in 1899. Only one year later, he was able to conclude his work and to submit his proposal to Congress.[44] However, the legislative procedure was lengthy and complex and the new Brazilian Civil Code was only passed sixteen years later, coming into force on 1 January 1917.

35. The Civil Code of 1916 (*Código Civil de 1916*, CC/1916) showed typical traces of nineteenth century mentality: it was shaped by individualism and liberalism; freedom of ownership and contract; as well as patriarchalism. Family law was particularly conservative resulting in criticism. *Pontes de Miranda*, an influential Brazilian lawyer[45] and the author of the sixty-volume commentary on the Brazilian Civil Code claimed that despite the fact that the code dated back to 1916, it shared the spirit of nineteenth century codification. According to him, the code was rather sophisticated but did not provide any solutions for current social issues.[46]

36. Major historical events in the twentieth century shaped Brazilian society, and new customs and traditions created new legal conditions. Life changed radically: large families (grandparents, father, mother, children, maid, etc.) living on farms turned into households of single parents or two fathers or two mothers and their children. The law of obligations also underwent key changes giving rise to demands among Brazilian lawyers to fundamentally reform the Civil Code.[47] The first attempt in the early 1960s failed when the drafts were withdrawn at the start of the military dictatorship in 1964.

42. Moreira Alves, A parte geral, p. 3.
43. Coelho Rodrigues, Projeto do Código Civil Brasileiro, 1980.
44. For details on creating the codification and its content, *see*: Beviláqua, Código Civil Commentado, 1944.
45. For the life and work of *Pontes de Miranda, see*: Schmidt, Vida e obra de Pontes de Miranda a partir de uma perspectiva alemã – com especial referência à tricotomia 'existência, validade e eficácia do negócio jurídico', RFDC, year 3, no. 5, pp. 135–158, 2014.
46. Pontes de Miranda, Einleitung, in: Heinsheimer (Hrsg.), Die Zivilgesetze der Gegenwart, Band III: Brasilien Código Civil, 1928.
47. Moreira Alves, A parte geral, pp. 3 ff.

37. In 1969, a new commission was nominated to review the 1916 Civil Code. However, the members of the commission headed by *Miguel Reale*[48] saw the need not merely to revise the existing code but rather to develop a new one. After thirty-three years, in January 2003, the new Brazilian Civil Code (*Código Civil de 2002*, CC/2002) entered into force with Law n° 10.406/02, constituting today's main source of Brazilian private law.

38. According to *Reale*, the most distinctive feature of the two civil codes is their philosophy: the 1916 Code was shaped by freedom of property and contract as well as patriarchalism and individualism while the current code adheres to the principles of *eticidade* (ethical values), *socialidade* (sociability), *operabilidade* (operativeness) and *concretude* (concreteness).[49]

39. The Brazilian Civil Code regulates most matters, although, as illustrated below, there are several supplementary statutes that take precedence over the civil code as they constitute specific legislation.[50]

40. A major difference between the 1916 and 2002 codes is the fact that the latter included company law and harmonized civil and commercial obligations. Although the 1850 Commercial Code is still valid, large parts of it have been repealed and replaced. Today it only applies to maritime trade.

41. However, consumer protection was not included in the 2002 Civil Code but is addressed in a supplementary statute (Law n° 8.078/90). Articles 2 and 3 of which, respectively, define the terms 'consumer' (*consumidor*) and 'supplier' (*fornecedor*) setting the law's target groups.[51]

---

48. Other members were *José Carlos Moreira Alves* (General Part), *Agostinho Alvim* (Law of Obligations), *Sylvio Marcondes* (Commercial Law), *Ebert Chamoun* (Property Law), *Clóvis do Couto e Silva* (Family Law) and *Torquato Castro* (Law of Succession).
49. For details on *Reale's* philosophy and guiding principles, *see*: Schmidt, Zivilrechtskodifikation in Brasilien, pp. 120 ff.: 'Das Leitprinzip der Eticidade trachte danach, den juristischen Formalismus, den das brasilianische Recht vom portugiesischen Recht und von der deutschen Pandektistik geerbt habe, zu überwinden. […] Demgegenüber habe man im CC/2002 an zahlreichen Stellen Vorschriften geschaffen, die die Einbeziehung ethischer Werte ermöglichen.' Bei dem Leitprinzip der Socialidade gehe es um 'Ausgleich individueller und kollektiver Interessen'. […] 'Mit dem Leitprinzip der Operabilidade verband Reale verschiedene Bedeutungen. Es gehe zunächst um Pragmatismus, um die Abschaffung unbegründeter Formalismen. […] Was die Concretitude angeht, meine es die Verpflichtung des Gesetzgebers, nicht von der Lebenswirklichkeit losgelöste Gesetze zu erlassen, sondern auf die konkreten sozialen Umstände eingehen.'
50. Feiten Wingert Ody, Die Kohärenz der Rechtsordnung des brasilianischen Privatrechts bezüglich des Schutzes der Schwächeren, in: Grundmann/Baldus/Herzog/Lebre de Freitas/Marques (Hrsg.), *Rechtssystem und Juristische Person – Sistema jurídico e pessoa jurídica*, Schriften zum Portugiesischen und Lusophonen Recht, 2012.
51. Feiten Wingert Ody, Lisiane. O conceito de consumidor e noção de vulnerabilidade nos países do Mercosul. In: *Revista de direito do consumidor*, v. 16, n. 64, pp. 80–108, out./dez., 2007. Also: Marques, Claudia; Bessa, Leonardo; Herman V. Benjamin, Antonio. *Manual de Direito do Consumidor*. São Paulo: RT, 2017. Cavalieri F°, Sérgio. *Programa de Direito do consumidor*. Rio de Janeiro: Atlas, 2019.

42. The Labour Code (*CLT*) applies to employment relationships and unites all labour laws. Additionally, there is a law on crimes against unfair banking practices (*Lei de Crimes contra a Economia Popular*) addressing usury (*lesão/usura*); and a law on renting (*Lei do Inquilinato*, Law n° 8.245/91) protecting tenants of urban residential properties (*imóvel residencial urbano*). The Child and Adolescent Statute (*Estatuto da Crianca e do Adolescente, ECA*) defends children and young people in matters such as adoption, guardianship, and violations of the law by them or against them (Law n° 8.069/90). The Statute of the Elderly (*Estatuto do Idoso*) comprises norms to protect senior citizens. They, for example, benefit from reduced proceeding's duration. Law n° 13.146/2015 was recently passed forming the Statute for Persons with Disabilities (*Estatuto da Pessoa com Deficiência*). It has changed the norms regarding disabled people in all legal spheres touching upon their legal capacity as well as fiscal obligations. These specific regulations prevail in relation to general legislation due to the particular situations the respective target groups are in.

43. As globalization proceeded, the relationships between the Brazilian government and the international market, as well as between Brazil and other nations, and on the private level between enterprises and workers changed considerably.

44. The contact and exchange between the nations as well as expanding international commerce led to extensive modifications in the legal sphere and a strong influence of the Anglo-American *Common Law* on the Brazilian legal system, requiring the adoption of a number of common law contracts.

45. Furthermore, the national legislator adopted some practices and concepts of the common law by including numerous General Clauses in the 2002 Code.

46. Additional general provisions in the law and recent changes to procedural law, which bind judges and courts in the lower courts to be guided by and interpret the decisions made in the higher courts, have caused a shift from codified law to case law in Brazilian legislation. Whereas laws used to originate from simple legal provisions, they now may be derived from judges' interpretations regarding general provisions and the guidelines provided by the higher courts. However, this causes a certain degree of legal uncertainty, because such court decisions do not always have a reasonable foundation or are not even based on legal provisions or precedents but rather on an appeal to authority.[52]

§3. The Primacy of Statute in the Brazilian Judicial System

47. Since Brazil's colonial period, it has been a tradition to give primacy to written law (Statute law). The Brazilian written normative system is built on the Federal Constitution, the *remaining core* of the national ordinance. Written law is the most important form of producing law in Brazil because it is considered the most

52. V. John Dawson, The General Clauses viewed from a distance. Rabels Z., 1977, 41/03, p. 441.

democratic, since the legislative power, in collaboration with the executive power, has the prerogative to both elaborate and sanction law.

48. Despite the existence of a number of references to customs as secondary sources of law or as a contract interpretation tool (Article 113 CC/02), these resources are still underused by Brazilian lawyers and judges.[53]

§4. Position of the Judiciary

49. The judicial branch is one of the powers of the Republic of Brazil, as stated in Article 2 of the Federal Constitution: *The Legislature, the Executive and the Judiciary, independent and harmonious among themselves, are the powers of the Union.*

50. According to Article 92 of the Federal Constitution, the bodies of the judicial branch are the following: the Supreme Federal Court (*Supremo Tribunal Federal–STF*); the National Council of Justice (*Conselho Nacional de Justiça – CNJ*); the Superior Court of Justice (*Superior Tribunal de Justiça–STJ*); the Federal Regional Courts and the Federal Judges (*Tribunais Regionais Federais e Juízes Federais*); the Labour Courts and Judges (*Tribunais e Juízes do Trabalho*); the Electoral Courts and Judges (*Tribunais e Juízes Eleitorais*); the Military Courts and Judges (*Tribunais e Juízes Militares*); and the Courts and Judges of the States, of the Federal District and of the Territories (*Tribunais e Juízes dos Estados e do Distrito Federal e Territórios*). The single paragraph of the same article adds that the Supreme Federal Court and the Superior Courts have their seats in the Federal District and their jurisdiction covers the entire Brazilian territory.

51. The judge's function is to apply the law, though not simply mechanically: he describes values and seeks the fairest solution, beginning by examining the facts and proof presented by the parties. The judge must make his or her decision carefully taking into consideration the entire juridical system, including the Federal Constitution and the norms of international treaties that Brazil has signed.

52. When faced by legal gaps in a specific case, the judge cannot refrain from taking a decision. He or she shall invoke the public customs, the analogy or the general principles of law.[54]

53. *See* Marcos de Campos Ludwig, Usos e Costumes no Processo Obrigacional, Editora Revista dos Tribunais, São Paulo, 2005.
54. Article 4 of the Introductory Law to the Civil Code.

53. The assemblage of court decisions forms case law (*jurisprudência*), which is not a primary or formal source of law in Brazil. However, it inspires judges and parties *as a source of knowledge that should repute itself in equal level to law and usage.*[55]

54. The Civil Code of 1916 and the Commercial Code of 1850 were updated by the interpretative work of judges and courts until their revocation.

55. The new Civil Code has incorporated a large part of the Commercial Code.[56] Due to its recent publication, the courts are interpreting it to create a harmonized understanding with respect to its innovations.

§5. Distinction Between Public Law and Private Law

56. Following the ancient Roman tradition, law was understood to be divided into two broad spheres: public and private law. With the extensive codifications introduced in the nineteenth (*Code Napoléon*) and twentieth (*Bürgerliches Gesetzbuch–BGB)* centuries and the adoption of political and economic liberalism, public law and private law became separated, so that public law rarely interfered in the private sphere, with the exception of some aspects such as family law and succession law.

57. However, along with the extenuation of the Liberal State, the classical distinction between the public and private spheres has diminished, leading to important political and economic changes and the increased influence of the private sphere on the public sphere. As a result, some aspects of private life began to be regulated or limited by the public sphere.

58. Over the last decade, *Pietro Perlingieri,* a Professor at Camerino University in Italy, has significantly influenced Brazilian legal doctrine. His writings and teachings have led some of his Brazilian disciples[57] to adopt a different conception of private law in Brazil, the so-called Civil-Constitutional Law, in which the constitution is placed at the centre of the system, embracing the areas of civil law (property, family and obligations), commercial law and consumer law.

59. This phenomenon is not new but rather results from factors such as the above-mentioned extenuation of the Liberal State and the disappearing distinction between public and private law, as well as the addition of provisions to the economic order to the Constitution, and the failure of private law to deal with issues such as bioethics.

---

55. *See* Karl Larenz, Derecho Civil-Parte General, Madrid, Editoriales de Derecho Reunidas, 1978, p. 16.
56. The Commercial Code from 1850 still regulates maritime trade.
57. For example, Maria Celina Bodin de Moraes, Luiz Edson Facchin (judge of the Supreme Court of Justice, STF) Gustavo Tepedino, Paulo Luiz Lobo Neto, Anderson Schereiber. The conceptions of these authors are not unanimously accepted by other scholars.

60. The 1988 Federal Constitution also affected economic activity, since it regulated the actions of free enterprise, established the principles of free competition and security, as well as its components, the legitimate reliance, the non-retroactivity of law, and the respect for the vested rights.

61. Furthermore, the Constitution has structured the basis of consumer relations in private law, offering a protective character to the respective regulatory laws.

62. The Constitutional Assembly in 1988 sought to extend regulation and protection to micro and small enterprises.

§6. Distinction Between Civil Law and Commercial Law

63. The first question that arises in this context concerns the continued validity of the distinction between civil and commercial law.

64. As Professor Jean Pierre Marty[58] has said, this exercise (the distinction between these two kinds of private law rules) may be unnecessary nowadays, because today it is more important to discuss the interference of public law on private law and the new disciplines that constitute economic and business law.

65. Despite the recognition of this phenomenon by the most important representatives of the French doctrine, there are jurists who still consider the distinction between civil and commercial law to be of great importance.

66. For eighty-six years, the Commercial Code of 1850 and the Civil Code of 1916 coexisted in Brazil, so traditionally, there was a distinction between the two. It is important to remark that besides the fact that the Commercial Code was older, some of its rules permitted a more flexible interpretation and application of the Civil Code.

67. Yet, the legislator of the 2002 Code, inspired by Italian doctrine and the Italian Civil Code of 1942, combined civil and commercial obligations and created an assemblage of rules concerning private companies and entrepreneurs, excluding only corporations, which are regulated by a special statute, namely Law n° 6.404/76. This law plays an important role, because the legislator considered it a subsidiary tool to be used in the case of there being any gap in the company law. Consequently, the Commercial Code remains in force, but exclusively with regard to maritime trade (Second Part of Law 556 of 1850).

---

58. G. Marty et P. Raynaud, Droit civil, Introduction générale à l'étude du droit, Sirey, 2nd édition, Paris, 1972.

68. According to the 2002 Civil Code, the regulation of companies and enterprises is intended to democratize them, while ensuring their necessary autonomy.[59]

69. It is important to highlight that, despite the unification of civil and commercial obligations, commercial law remains autonomous from civil law, because the unification is of a legislative nature and does not modify the essence of these branches. Each conserves its own nature and essence. The only real innovation provided by the new code is the introduction of the concepts of the enterprise (*empresa*) and the businessman (*empresário*) and the substitution of the traditional concepts of the *commercial act* (*ato de comércio*) by enterprise, and *goodwill* (*fundo de comércio*) by *establishment* (*estabelecimento*).

70. The Civil Code classifies both associations (*associações*) and corporations (*sociedades*) as private regardless of their form. The only exceptions are *simple* corporations (*sociedade simples*) whose activities are economic but not commercial or connected to a business organization. A business corporation is economically organized, and its aim is the production or circulation of goods or services, according to Article 966 of the Civil Code.

---

59. Miguel Reale, Estudos preliminares do Código Civil, São Paulo, Editora Revista dos Tribunais, 2003, p. 83.

Introduction to the Law of Contracts

§1. Definition of Contract

71. A contract (*contrato*) is an agreement in conformity with the law which is intended to facilitate the acquisition, protection, transferral, conservation, modification or extinction of rights.[60]

§2. Historical Background of the Law of Contracts

72. While the concept of a contract under Brazilian law has been influenced by various legal systems, that of the Romans is the strongest since it also had a profound impact on Portuguese colonial law that defined Brazilian law. Notably, the legislator of the 1916 Civil Code admired Roman civilization and the way their society was organized by norms that are still in force in many systems today. Obviously, the Roman concept of contracts was updated when it was included in the 1916 Civil Code. These changes concerned, above all, the numerous formalities of Roman law and the way creditors executed their rights that in Roman law were executed on the person of the debtor (*Lex Poetelia Papiria*). In all modern Civil Codes (*Code Napoléon* and *BGB*) this form was replaced by the execution on the debtor's goods and assets.

73. In addition, Brazilian law was influenced by French concepts inspired by rules from the *Code Napoléon*, especially in the field of liability and contracts.

74. Another relevant factor to consider when analysing the concept of a contract is the economic and political environment. That is to say, the private autonomy expressed in the contract can be stronger or weaker depending on the degree of liberalism and individualism in force in the society and the political sphere.

75. For almost forty years, the Brazilian private law system was independent of the public law because the non-communication between the two is a characteristic of liberalism in law. For this reason, it used to be called a 'closed system' in Brazilian legal doctrine, in contrast to an 'open system' such as in the common law systems.

60. Caio Mário, *Instituições de Direito Civil*, Editora Forense, Rio de Janeiro, vol. III, p. 7.

76. According to the concept of a closed legal system, the responses to all problems of a certain society can be found within it. The judge does not need to look for solutions in other systems. If the law, however, fails to regulate certain issues, the judge has a legal tool to fill the gap: according to Article 4 of the introductory law to the Civil Code, he or she has to apply the general principles of law, the customs and the analogy to solve the problem.

77. In an open system the judge can find the solution to a legal problem outside of the national law system and looks into morals, customs, social values, etc. to solve a conflict.

78. Traditionally, continental European systems and South American legal systems used to be closed.

79. When liberalism was abandoned, the closed system was obliged to open up: judges could not find the solutions to newly emerging issues within the changing local society that the Code did not foresee, so they were obliged to resort to solutions from outside the system. The reasons for these gaps in the Code's rules were the changes in Brazilian society due to industrialization, migration from the countryside into cities and the entry of women into the workforce. The most important factor for this development, however, was the shift in social attitudes in Brazilian society. People began to accept and concede rights to couples who lived together without being legally married. This new phenomenon was called a 'stable union' (*união estável*), a neologism created in the Brazilian doctrine and adopted by judges and courts.

80. At the end of the 1970s, an important author, Professor Clóvis do Couto e Silva, began to elaborate a new concept of obligation inspired by the German concept. It was called '*obligation as a Process*' ('*obrigação como processo*') and regarded the relationship between parties as being based on cooperative behaviour. This point of view was very different from the traditional Brazilian outlook on this subject, which was based on the French Code from 1804, in which parties were considered rather as opponents than as partners.

81. At the same time, and again influenced by the German doctrine, the Brazilian doctrine and courts acknowledged that the *obligation as a process* was regulated by the principle of good faith regarding the person's behaviour. This new concept of obligations and contracts led to a revolution in Brazilian private law. Since then it has undergone permanent evolution and has been updated by theories from scholars and judges.

82. The Constitution of 1988 also profoundly modified the concept of contracts in Brazilian Law, because it introduced the consumer relationship as a new kind of juridical relationship and obliged the legislative power to develop a Consumer Protection Code, which was eventually created by Law n° 8.078 on 11 September 1990.

83. This new kind of contract involving consumers has its roots in mass behaviour, a concept that is absent from the traditional rules of contract. Today, minors, entirely or partially disabled persons and people with full legal capacity can purchase for consumption. Therefore, the legislator has created special rules, according to which the consumer is a weaker party and the trader or supplier a stronger party. The legislator of the Consumer Protection Code was inspired by the EEC Directive from 1985 on the *manufacturer's liability for defective products* and other similar documents, such as the Louisiana Consumer legislation.

84. Since the Consumer Protection Code was passed, there have been two types of contracts in Brazilian law: civil code contracts, with parties considered equal; and consumer contracts, in which the parties, as mentioned above, are not equals, because the stronger party has greater economic power and more knowledge about the goods in question, while the other party does not have that power and is thus vulnerable.

85. The Consumer Protection Code is a good example of this opening of the legal system which began with the decline of liberalism and the growing impact of the state in private relationships.

§3. Classification of Contracts

86. Authors may classify contracts differently depending on their conception or perspective. We will do it in a practical (or pragmatic) sense.

I. Formation and Effects: Unilateral/Non-synallagmatic and Bilateral/Synallagmatic Contracts

87. Unilateral contracts (*contrato unilateral/não-sinalagmático*) create obligations for only one of the parties, e.g., donations and loans for use (*comodato*).

88. Bilateral contracts (*contrato bilateral/sinalagmático*) obliges both parties to perform obligations and exercise rights, e.g., sales contracts: on the one hand, the seller has an obligation to transfer the good to the buyer who has to pay for it; on the other hand, the seller has the right to be paid and the buyer to become the good's owner.

89. The Greek expression *synallagmatic* indicates the existence of a nexus or synallagma between the parties meaning that each obligation is the reason for the other. This classification is crucial, especially since some remedies are only applicable to certain types of contracts. For instance, *the exceptio non adimpleti contractus* can only be invoked in synallagmatic contracts.

II. Requirements of Form: Formal and Informal Contracts

90. The law can regulate how the parties sign their contract. Therefore, there is a distinction between formal (*contrato solene/formal*) and informal contracts (*contrato sem forma específica/informal/forma livre*).

91. Formal contracts may have two different purposes: first, to ensure the security of the contract, and second, to prove its existence. Under Roman law, it was necessary to follow a standard procedure in any legal transaction, because formalism was the means to guarantee the security of such acts. Nowadays, requirements of form are mostly used to prove the existence of a contract. Most contracts are not formal but simply consensual, so they are formed based on each party's willingness to participate.

III. Relationship of Dependency: Principal and Accessory Contracts

92. A principal contract (*contrato principal*) does not depend on any other contract but stands by itself, such as the contract for the sale of a car.

93. Accessory contracts (*contrato acessório*), however, depend on the existence of another contract, such as the payment of interests or warranties.

94. There is an ancient Roman rule that says: *the accessory follows the principal* meaning that all the events that affect the principal contract will affect the accessory contract as well. For instance, when a loan agreement comes to an end, the payment of interests can no longer be imposed.

IV. Moment of the Formation: Consensual and Real Contracts

95. In Brazilian law, there are two ways to acquire goods and/or services: the most common being 'consensual contracts' (*contrato consensual*), which involve the exchange of declarations of will, and the other being 'real contracts' (*contrato real*), on the formation of which, for security reasons, the law imposes the transmission as a second requisite. When the purpose of the contract is to transfer the property of a corporeal thing, as in the case for sales contracts, the possession needs to be transferred. If the contract's purpose is to transfer real estate, the agreement must be registered in the Real Estate Record (*Registro de Imóveis*).

V. Time of Performance: Instantaneous and Continuous Performance

96. Contracts of instantaneous performance (*contrato de execução instantânea*) are completed in and by a single act, even when the consideration is performed sometime after the contractual bond. In the latter case, such contracts are also called contracts of delayed performance (*contrato de execução diferida*).

97. In addition, there are contracts which are performed continuously, such as work contracts (*trato sucessivo*). This classification is important because there are different consequences in the case of a breach of contract: if one of the parties infringes a contract of instantaneous performance the parties return to the state as if the contract had never existed; but, if the contract is performed continuously, the effects produced by the contract prior to the breach remain unaffected by the breach.

VI. Existence of the Reciprocal Benefits: Commutative and Aleatory Contracts

98. In commutative contracts (*contrato comutativo*), each of the contracting parties gives and receives an equivalent, as it happens in sale's contracts (according to Black's Law Dictionary, Centennial Edition 1891–1991).

99. According to Black's Law Dictionary, a contract is aleatory (*contrato aleatório*) when it contains a mutual agreement, the effects of which, regarding both the advantages and losses to all parties or some of them, depend on an uncertain event. Under the terms of the French doctrine, when the contract is aleatory, the competing parties are exposed to the possibility of profit or loss. The doctrine considers the insurance contract to be aleatory, as well as the obligation to pay annuities. In Brazil, however, some authors, such as Professor Judith Martins-Costa, disagree with this general point of view concerning the nature of insurance contracts and consider them to be commutative.[61]

100. According to Brazilian doctrine, contracts on life pensions (Article 803 CC/02) and gambling (Article 814 CC/02) as well as those that involve an element of fortuity or jeopardy are aleatory.

101. This classification is especially relevant in relation to economic loss, because the rules of economic loss can be applied only to commutative contracts. Economic loss is characterized by a disproportion between the considerations (*desproporção das prestações*, Article 157 CC/02).

102. The existence of a redhibitory defect or vice (*vícios redibitórios*) can only be invoked in commutative contracts. In aleatory contracts, the parties cannot require the other party to pay an earnest money deposit to ensure the fulfilment of the obligations of the contract (*arras*).

---

61. Judith Martins-Costa, *A Boa-Fé e o Seguro no Novo Código Civil Brasileiro* (virtualidades da boa-fé como regra e como cláusula geral). In: III Fórum de Direito do Seguro. São Paulo: Manuais Técnicos de Seguros – IBDS, 2003, p. 59. *See also*: Fábio S. de Andrade, 'O desenvolvimento do contrato de seguro no direito civil brasileiro atual'. In: *Revista de Derecho Privado,* Universidad Externado de Colombia, n. 28, January-June 2015, pp. 203–236. DOI: 10.18601/01234366.

VII. Typical and Atypical Contracts

103. Contracts can also be divided into standardized contracts (*contrato típico*) that are regulated by the law, such as contracts regarding sales, donations, loans, etc. and other contracts that are not legally standardized (*contrato atípico*) and have their roots in the principle of the autonomy of will that is present in the social environment, allowing the parties to freely create legal relations as long as they do not breach the limits of the juridical order. Some authors refer to the same devices as nominate contracts (*contrato nominado*) and innominate contracts (*contrato inominado*), respectively.

104. Another factor that has led to the increasing use of atypical contracts is the global circulation of juridical models. Due to globalization and new means of communication, a considerable number of contractual types from foreign legal systems, such as the common law, have been introduced to Brazil, e.g., contracts on *franchising, shopping centres, factoring, turn-key, engineering, catering, parking, etc.*

VIII. Civil and Commercial Contracts

105. The distinction between civil (*contrato civil*) and commercial contracts (*contrato comercial*) is subject to debate due to the controversial element of the commercial act (*ato de comércio*).

106. It is possible to say that the same contract, according to its economic aims, could be civil or commercial, considering the quality of the parties, as the subjectivist doctrine (*doutrina subjetivista*) teaches. According to this doctrine only people practising certain commercial acts which were considered as such were allowed to be recognized as business people. Although the doctrine was forgotten for decades, it is reviving now.

107. However, it is necessary to stress that there are contracts whose nature is essentially civil, like donations, and others whose nature is essentially commercial, like work contracts and company mergers and divisions.

108. Some law systems have unified civil and commercial obligations, as is the case in Switzerland and the European Union which today have a Code of Civil and Commercial Obligations. Nevertheless, it is important to distinguish between them because their interpretation is rather different and they are regulated by different rules in Brazilian law.

IX. Transferability: Personal Service Contracts and Non-personal Service Contracts

109. Sometimes, the qualities of the contracting parties are very important. The right choice of the person to carry out a certain task, for instance, a painting by a specific artist, or a meal prepared by a particular chef de cuisine, is fundamental (*intuitu personae*).

110. In other cases, the choice of the contracted party does not depend on his or her qualities but only on their ability to execute the contract, such as the choice of a painter to paint the walls of a house (*not intuitu personae*).

111. Nevertheless, sometimes it may occur that a contract that at the outset of its formation was not *intuitu personae* becomes *intuitu personae*. For example, when one party contracts someone, for instance, a sales manager to work in a factory, but some years later the sales manager is replaced, after which the buyer refuses to deal with the new sales manager and states he will only deal with the former sales manager.

112. This kind of distinction is also important, when one party dies. If the contract is *intuitu personae*, the contract is over; if it is not, the heirs are compelled to execute the contract. The contract cannot be reassigned.

113. Incidentally, a work contract is an intermediate category because the worker's personal qualities are not always required.

X. Drafting: Adhesion Contracts

114. The adhesion contract (*contrato de/por adesão*) is one of the most widely discussed and controversial kinds of contract. It is a common, contemporaneous way of reaching contractual agreements, whereby only one of the contracting parties drafts the contract using standardized clauses avoiding any kind of negotiation regarding the form or content prior to the formation of the contract while the other has to accept it, otherwise the parties do not contract. In the field of consumer law, one expression that summarizes this special contract is '*Take it or leave it!*'

115. From the perspective of the party that drafts the clauses of the contract, according to some authors, the contract proposal is called 'General Conditions of Business' (*condições gerais do negócio*). One might raise the question as to why after the formation of the contractual relationship, the exact same relation is called an adhesion contract: according to Professor Garcia Amico, these dissimilar denominations correspond to two logically and chronologically distinct moments of the same phenomenon. Another interesting aspect of this type of contract is that general conditions of business can be accepted individually by several people without creating any connection between them.

116. The Brazilian doctrine and case law, under French influence, prefer the expression 'adhesion contract' to 'General Conditions of Business' as used in Germany and in Portugal. Although some scholars consider these two denominations synonymous, the expression 'adhesion contract' is more limited than the 'General Conditions of Business'.

117. The Brazilian Consumer Protection Code regulates adhesion contracts in Article 54 and paragraphs.

118. The most common adhesion contracts are the supply of transport, energy, water and telephone services, as well as bank contracts, maritime contracts and contracts on the sale of goods. Some adhesion contracts relate to administrative law, such as contracts on collective transportation and the supply of water and energy.

XI. Standard-Form Contracts

119. Standard-form contracts (*condições gerais do negócio*) are very similar to adhesion contracts in terms of their form and function. A standard-form contract is used when the future parties belong to opposite and organized professional categories, for instance, breweries and beer retailers or enterprises.

120. The structure of the standard-form contract is usually the result of cooperation between both parties.

121. Generally, the interested party organizes its relationships under these kinds of contracts, because the parties are not obliged to establish a concrete form of contract.

122. The main obligation the contracting parties have is to conclude the deals founded on the requests that both parties have made to each other.[62]

§4. Contract and Torts

123. For a long time, the doctrine has distinguished between contractual (*responsabilidade contratual*) and extra-contractual liability (*responsabilidade extracontratual*). Contractual liability results from the violation of a credit right or an obligation in a technical sense, as expressed by Mário Julio de Almeida Costa. This author pointed out that the nomenclature used by the doctrine in this field is not appropriate, because besides contracts, there are other sources of liability, like the unilateral declaration of will (*ato unilateral de vontade*); even the law can be a

62. There are many books by different authors on this classification, among which we would like to refer to Orlando Gomes, Contratos, Editora Forense, Rio de Janeiro, 1991, 12th edition, and Arnoldo Wald, Obrigações e Contratos, Editora Saraiva, São Paulo, 2004, 16th edition.

source of liability. For this reason, Professor Almeida Costa prefers the term 'obligational liability' (*responsabilidade obrigacional*).[63]

124. There are some legal requirements for a contractual liability,[64] such as valid contract and damage (*prejuízo, dano*) that results from the non-performance of an obligation of the contract and is connected to the victim. The doctrine does not unanimously agree on the requirement of the existence of a contractual liability (*responsabilidade contratual*). Indeed, some scholars consider non-performance of a contractual obligation as sufficient grounds for contractual liability.[65] Others argue that only in the case of a violation of the main obligation is the point of view acceptable.

125. Sometimes, the courts add or deduce an obligation that the parties or even the law did not foresee, such as the obligation to give more information or even to warn the other party.[66]

126. Non-contractual liability results from the breach of a duty of conduct, which all members of the community have to observe. It concerns respect for absolute rights, such as the right to life, honour, physical integrity, etc. Accordingly, Article 186 of the Brazilian Civil Code governs that the person who violates someone's rights or harms another person, even morally, by an action or by voluntary omission, by negligence or imprudence, commits an illicit act.

127. The current Civil Code regulates non-contractual liability in Articles 186, 188, 927 and 954, and contractual liability in Articles 389 and 395. Nevertheless, the Code does not refer to any difference between those two kinds of liability. Moreover, it regulates neither liability that emerges from the non-performance of the obligation nor liability resulting from the defective performance or delayed performance of the contractual obligations (the rules of which are in the chapter concerning the non-performance of obligations (Chapter 5. Termination of Contract and Chapter 6. Remedies)).

128. Obviously, contractual liability also encompasses the non-performance or the delayed performance of any kind of obligation, even when the source is a unilateral affair, like the power of attorney, a promised reward, or the law, such as the obligation to pay alimony.

---

63. Direito das Obrigações, 6th edição, 1994, Livraria Almedina, Coimbra, 1994, pp. 450 et seq.
64. The expression 'contractual liability' appears in 1892 in Jean Grandmoulin's book *De l'unité de la responsabilité ou nature délictuelle de la responsabilité pour violation d'une obligation contractuelle*, where breach of contract is, for the first time, considered a source of liability.
65. V. Geneviève Viney, La Responsabilité contractuelle en question, Études offertes à Jacques Ghestin, Le contrat au début du XXè. Siècle, LGDJ, Paris, 2001, p. 921; Denis Tallon, Pourquoi parler de faute contractuelle? Études en l'honneur de Gérard Cornu, PUF, Paris, 1994, p. 429. By the same author L'inéxecution du contrat: pour une autre présentation, RTDciv., 1994, p. 223.
66. Véra Jacob de Fradera, Informar ou não informar, eis a questão, in Estudos de Direito Privado e Processual Civil, em Homenagem a Clóvis do Couto e Silva, org. by Judith Martins-Costa e Vera Jacob de Fradera, Editora Revista dos Tribunais, São Paulo, 2014, pp. 231 et seq., especial pp. 245–251.

129. Non-contractual liability includes the breach of some general duties, such as real estate or personality rights or authors' rights.

130. While there are aspects common to both kinds of liability, there are also characteristics peculiar to contractual liability, such as the *exception non adimpleti contractus*. Article 476 of the Brazilian Civil Code states that in bilateral contracts no party is allowed to demand the fulfilment of the obligation by the other party before fulfilling its own obligation;

131. Article 475 CC/02 further establishes that the party harmed by the breach can choose the dissolution of the contract, unless it prefers that the contract be executed by the other party. In any case, a compensation for damages and losses is due.

132. In the following section, we will point out the most relevant differences between these two kinds of liability.

I. Burden of Proof (*ônus da prova*)

133. In the field of contractual liability, the creditor must prove any non-compliance with the obligation (*inadimplemento da obrigação*). In this case, the debtor must – if possible – demonstrate that he or she did not comply with the obligation for one of the exclusive reasons admitted by the law: the victim's fault (creditor) or Force Majeure (*força maior*) or an Act of God (*caso fortuito*).

134. In the field of non-contractual liability, the claimant has to prove that the damage occurred as a consequence of the unlawful behaviour of the party that caused the damage.

II. Differences Concerning the Capacity of the Tortfeasor

135. Concerning the matter of contractual liability, the party's capacity depends on the observance of some conditions. For instance, the person who wants to be part of a contract needs to be legally capable, because legal capacity is a condition imposed by the law for this kind of affair. If a minor wants to enter into a contract, he or she can do so through a representative, such as a parent or a tutor. If a minor maliciously affirms that he or she is of age, the Civil Code states in Article 180 that the minor between 16 and 18 years cannot invoke his age with the intent to be discharged from an obligation, if he or she intentionally hid it when asked by the other party, or – when obliging – he or she declared to be capable.

136. In the case of torts caused by an incapable person, the person legally responsible for this incapable person can be obliged to repair the harm caused by the unlawful action.

137. It must be stressed that there is a new tendency in Brazilian law to increase the liability of incapable persons, as written in Article 928 CC/02.[67]

III. Graduation of the Fault

138. In general, both kinds of civil liability are grounded on the presence of a fault.

139. Contractual liability can be graded, according to the different situations in which the fault occurred. The Civil Code does not distinguish between a *light* fault and *very light* fault, and this difference is implicit. The patterns of conduct that are accepted are the '*bon père de famille*' and the 'reasonable man'.

140. In the case of non-contractual liability, the fault is evaluated more rigorously and thoroughly covering even very light faults.

141. The liability can be subjective, i.e., grounded on a fault, and objective, i.e., grounded on the existence of damage related to a certain action or activity (risk created and risk profit) of an agent or an enterprise, independently of the fault. Currently, fault is no longer the only ground for liability.

142. We can conclude this section by noting that until the beginning of the nineteenth century, civil liability was a relatively unimportant matter, whereas today, by contrast, it tends to touch all fields of human life. Accordingly, the dominant concept in the legal literature of those times, was *all the law is in the contract ('Tout le droit est dans le contrat'),* now it has changed to *all the law is in the civil liability (aujourd'hui tout le droit est dans la responsabilité civile).*

143. In summary, we can see a return to the origins of civil liability, as an element related to morality and religion, in the period of the *non-droit*, as suggested by Carbonnier,[68] grounded on the principles of trust and good faith. The Swiss and German doctrines concerning pre-contractual liability are proof of that. Indeed, both recognize this special liability founded on a breach of trust before the conclusion of a contract; and both accept the *variae causarum figurae modernae* as their origin, which Gaius was the first to discover.

---

67. Article 928 CC. The non-capable individual is liable for the damages he or she causes, if the persons responsible for him or her do not have the duty or sufficient means to do so. Paragraph. The indemnity foreseen in this article shall be equitable and not due if it deprives the non-capable person or the persons depending on him or her of their necessities.
68. Le Flexible Droit, LGDJ, Paris, 1963, pp. 9–74.

§5. Contracts and Quasi-Contracts

144. Brazilian law does not recognize the concept of a quasi-contract. Related issues are dealt with under §8 in Chapter 6 (Restitution).

§6. Contracts and Law of Property

145. *See* above, Introduction to the Law of Contracts, §3, IV.

§7. Contracts and Trust

146. Brazilian law has not adopted the concept of trust as such, but a few scholars are trying to introduce it into the national legal system.[69] However, there are some kinds of contract that are similar to the concept of trust, like fiduciary contracts (*negócios fiduciários*). There is also a draft law (nº 4.809), proposed by Deputy José Chaves and dating from 1998, which intends to introduce the contract of *fiducia* to the Brazilian legal system.

§8. Good Faith (*Boa-Fé*) and Fair Dealing

147. Article 422 of the Brazilian Civil Code states that the contracting parties shall, at the conclusion of the contract, as well as during their performance, adhere to the principles of probity and good faith. This norm immediately raises the question of the real nature of good faith and whether it is a standard or general principle. Some legal systems consider it a standard, like a judgment criterion, while others regard it as a principle and therefore emphasize it.

148. Depending on the matter, standard good faith can have many varied meanings because the standard is based on factual measurements without any biased judgment or analysis.

149. According to the French law professor Béatrice Jaluzot, good faith is a concept of a variable geometry and doubtful constancy, but whose advantage is its flexibility. Two good examples of this concept are the *Code Napoléon* and the Uniform Commercial Code of the USA.

150. As a principle, good faith plays three roles: interpretation, concretization and control.

69. Melhim Namem Chaloub, Trust, Perspectivas do Direito Contemporâneo na Transmissão da Propriedade para administração de Investimentos e Garantia, Editora Renovar, Rio de Janeiro, São Paulo, 2001; Rodrigo Garcia da Fonseca, Considerações sobre o Trust (Fidúcia) no Direito Comparado, Revista Forense, Rio de Janeiro, vol. 334, pp. 153–190, abr./jun. 1996; Martins-Costa, Judith, Os Negócios Fiduciários: Considerações sobre a Possibilidade de Acolhimento do Trust no Direito Brasileiro, Revista dos Tribunais, v. 657, São Paulo: Editora Revista dos Tribunais, 1990, pp. 37–50.

151. With regard to the interpretative function of good faith, Article 113 in the general part of the Civil Code states that legal affairs must be interpreted pursuant to the good faith and the traditions of their place of formation.

152. Concerning the control function, Brazilian law considers good faith as a directive on the parties' behaviour during the performance of the contract. This directive allows the judge to effectively control their behaviour. As we can see, the exercise of private autonomy in Brazilian law may be controlled under the terms of Article 422 of the Civil Code that obliges the parties to adhere to the principles of probity and good faith during all phases of the contract (formation and performance).

153. Related to the sanction against the abuse of rights, similar to sanctions imposed against violation of the principle of good faith, there is significant French influence, represented by the finalist doctrine of Louis Josserand, which considers the abusive exercise of a right to be an illicit act. Nevertheless, this understanding of the abuse of rights is not unanimously shared.

154. Good faith is widely discussed in Brazilian doctrine, because sometimes, it may be understood as a standard or as a principle. Regarding this discussion, we can affirm that the concept of good faith is employed in various fields of Brazilian law, such as commercial law, administrative law, public law, consumer law, etc. The understanding of the concept is not new, since good faith was considered an underlying principle in the former Civil Code (1916–2002). In the current Civil Code, good faith is foreseen in Articles 113 and 422.

155. In addition, Brazilian judges have developed a range of duties grounded on good faith with the purpose of fulfilling the content of the contract between the parties.

From this perspective, good faith is considered a Praetorian creation which was inspired by German legal literature and jurisprudence.

156. In fact, in German law, all accessory obligations are grounded on the principle of good faith (§§ 157 and 242 BGB). A long time ago, German judges created very specific obligations that are similar to real material rules. According to this doctrine, in the Law of Obligations, the parties have to observe three relevant categories of duties: cooperation, information and protection. From these duties, other duties emerge, such as *Treuepflicht* (fidelity duty), which is only applicable to commercial and labour contracts. In Brazilian law, the cooperative conception of the contract consists of a peculiar understanding conceived as a mechanism of interconnected links, which can be detached from each other without affecting the whole. The secondary duties (*deveres secundários*) emerge from the main obligation (*dever principal*), as well as the accessory and ancillary duties (*deveres laterais ou anexos*) that relate to mutual cooperation and collaboration. In certain cases, they may stand independently from any other obligation. The performance of these duties contributes to a better execution of the main obligation which is dealt with in the book by Clóvis do Couto e Silva *The Obligation as a Process*.[70]

157. It is important to refer to the distinct terminology employed by French law in comparison to Brazilian and German law, especially concerning the consequences of the principle of good faith in contractual relationships: while French lawyers and judges use the expression accessory obligations (*obligations accessoires*), German and Brazilian prefer the term duties (*Nebenpflichten / deveres laterais ou anexos*). The reason for this difference in understanding originates in the conception of accessory duties as rules that the parties did not agree upon in terms of the contract, because they only agreed on the terms of the main obligation. The parties cannot ignore the principle of good faith in their contractual relationship.

§9. Style of Drafting

158. Generally, legal systems present two main types of juridical rules: compelling (or constraining or binding) norms and permissive norms, which do not contain a command (or an order) to do or not to do something, but consent in the practice of certain acts, whose execution is authorized by legal order.

159. In juridical science, there is a distinction between different degrees of imperativeness: the imperative rules, which cannot be modified by the parties or by the judge, and the dispositive rules, a special kind of obligatory rule that grants freedom to parties. In Brazilian law, the dispositive rules have two purposes: first, they regulate the relation between the parties when they could have specified their interests but remained silent. For example, people who want to marry need to choose a matrimonial regime to regulate property ownership between spouses before their marriage. If they fail to do so, the law says that their regime will be the '*Comunhão Parcial de Bens*' (partial community property), whereby (a) the premarital property of each spouse remains the personal property of such spouse together with any property purchased during the marriage using resources or rights which predate the marriage and (b) property acquired after the marriage is owned jointly. Second, dispositive rules are related to situations in which a person exercises his or her right granted by law incompletely. For example, Brazilian law allows the testator to make monetary donations to poor people in his or her will. If, however, the testator does not inform to whom he or she wants to offer such a donation, the law adds that the donation will be transmitted to the poor people of the place where the testator was living during the last years of his or her life. These two examples demonstrate that the dispositive rules are also compelling and apply when the interested person remains silent (first case) or even when he or she speaks but does so incompletely (second case). In the first case, this rule is called a 'suppletive dispositive norm' (*norma dispositiva supletiva*); in the second case, it is called 'interpretative dispositive norm' (*norma dispositiva interpretativa*).

---

70. Couto E Silva, Clóvis: A obrigação como processo. São Paulo: Bushatski, 1976.

160. As Professor Lydia Belotsky has pointed out, little attention has been paid to the question of the relations between the normative style and the authoritative power of different types of rules. This subject is very important because these relationships must be clarified and the doctrine needs to analyse their impact on the ability of legal systems to adapt to a changing world or to induce a social change.[71]

161. We begin this matter by presenting the classification of legal rules. There are constraining or binding rules and non-binding norms. As stressed by Professor Riccardo Guastini, a rule or norm will be considered constraining (or compelling) if, and only if, it is at the same time imperative or mandatory and precise in its formulation (requiring a definite behaviour from a definite subject in definite circumstances and supported by another rule providing a sanction in case of infringement of the first rule).[72] Therefore, non-compelling or permissive norms do not contain any command or order to do or not to do something, but consent to the practice of certain acts, whose execution is authorized by the legal order.

162. Another relevant aspect concerning the style of Brazilian law concerns the detailed items of an article of law. Some lists enumerated in articles may have a purely exemplifying quality, whereas the enumeration of other rules may present an exhaustive character, not allowing any other hypotheses to be added to the list.

163. The legislator of the Brazilian Civil Code does not distinguish very often, nor very well between rules containing a dispositive norm and norms containing a merely exemplary or exhaustive enumeration. Given these characteristics, the interpreter needs some other assisting rules from the code to interpret the law well. One of the most important rules in this regard is Article 4 of the Introductory Law of the Civil Code, which was mentioned above, which is now known as the *Lei de Introdução às Normas do Direito brasileiro* (Introductory Act to the Rules of the Brazilian Law; Lei 12.376/2010). According to the article, the social aims of the law must be taken into account. In addition, doctrine and case law are important guides when interpreting the law, despite the fact they are not sources of law in the Brazilian system.

164. Laws can also be classified by their sanctions. In this sense, the doctrine classifies the norms as perfect, imperfect and more than perfect norms. Perfect norms (*normas perfeitas*) are those in which the sanctions correspond exactly to the gravity of the conduct imposed by the rule; imperfect norms (*normas imperfeitas*) have weak sanctions relative to the violation; and more than perfect norms (*normas mais que perfeitas*) impose double sanctions, such as a penalty and the obligation to return a good to its owner, which is the case for the delict of robbery.

---

71. Belotsky, Lydia. *'The style of legislation: narrative norms and Constraining Norms'*. In: Israeli reports to the XIV International Congress of Comparative Law, Athens, 1994, Giuffrè, 1994, pp. 29–41.
72. Guastini, Riccardo. Compelling and Non-Compelling Normative Formulations. In: Italian National Reports to the XIV International Congress of Comparative Law, Athens, 1994, Giuffrè, 1994, pp. 32–47.

165. At the Congress of the International Comparative Law Academy (IACL) held in Athens, Greece in August 1994, Professor Erik Jayme proposed a new classification of the legal rules, that he called 'narrative norms' (*normas narrativas*). These norms narrate and describe without imposing viable consequences for non-compliance with their terms, for example, the right to have a home, which is fundamental.

166. The former Brazilian Civil Code, published in 1916, was greatly inspired by these older laws. It was a patriarchal and individualist code in accordance with Brazilian society at that time, but it allowed the opening of the law under certain circumstances. This matter recognizes a phenomenon of a rather recent origin in the process of legislation and concerns the transition of style from a more traditional form of statutory command backed by sanctions and penalties.

167. A part of the Brazilian doctrine accepted this new classification, including the authors of this monograph, but most of the national lawyers and judges, that do not follow the progress in comparative law, do not recognize this new classification of juridical norms.

168. The complementary Law n° 95 from February 1998, which exposes the rules of the elaboration of law, its drafting, modification and consolidation according to Article 59 of the Federal Constitution comprises a chapter on Preliminary Dispositions (I); on the Techniques of Elaboration, Drafting and Modification of the Laws (II); and on the Consolidation of Law and Other Regulatory Acts (III), as well as Final Dispositions (IV).

§10. Sources of the Law of Contracts

169. As a country in which Europeans – in this case the Portuguese – settled, the first Brazilian sources of law were the *Ordenações do Reino* that were referred to in the introduction of this monograph.

170. Besides these sources, the settlers acknowledged other sources of law of subsidiary and complementary value like Roman and Canon law as well as customary rules.

171. As Pontes de Miranda said, our law does not come from the seeds, but from a branch planted by the Portuguese settler. (…) It is very important to follow the evolution of Brazilian law before it became a colony. That is the only way to understand the phenomena that will happened subsequently.[73]

172. Raymundo Faoro,[74] the author of several important books and articles about the juridical and political Brazilian evolution, stresses that the Portuguese law

73. Fontes e Evolução do Direito Civil Brasileiro, Forense, Rio de Janeiro, 1981, p. 28.
74. Os Donos do Poder, editora Globo, Porto Alegre, 1973.

preferred to organize the State politically, instead of developing commerce and economy. Another deep preoccupation of the settlers was the regulation of social relationships by general rules instead of rules that were only valid in every individual case. This thought coincided with the need to increase the king's authority, to ensure that he was stronger and had more privileges than the nobles and clergy. In its essential aspects, Portuguese law was founded on Roman law. Still, it does not constitute a *real* code, but rather a consolidation of rules, i.e., a mixture of various influences like Canon law and Arab and Visigothic customs. Obviously, there were many gaps in this consolidation, due to which the glosses of Accursius[75] and Bartolo's opinions[76] were applied.

173. In 1769, the Portuguese government published the *Law of Good Reason*[77] (*Lei da Boa Razão*), the *recta ratio*, that forbade the use of the glosses of Accursius and Bartolo's opinions to fill the gaps in the system.

174. As Clóvis do Couto e Silva said, in §9 of the *Law of Good Reason*, the legislator considered that it held the fundamental principles containing the intrinsic and permanent essential truths, established by the Roman Ethics, inserted in Roman and Natural Law.

175. In this context, one of the most interesting characteristics of Brazilian law becomes evident: the use of foreign law to fill the gaps in the national system. In ancient times, the *foreign law* was the *Law of Good Reason*, as well as the *Subsidiary Law*. Till today, Brazilian courts and attorneys have resorted to foreign solutions to solve national problems. According to the doctrine, the *Law of Good Reason* served as a general clause, providing the opportunity for the Brazilian law system to be open other ways to do justice. As can be seen, our sources of law have been open since colonial times, and they remain so until today.

176. The most important source of law in Brazil is the law considered as the expression of the general will, as stated in the Declaration of the Rights of Man and of the Citizen (1791).

---

75. The glosses are notations, generally very short, about a legal text, intended to explain the sense of one word. In the thirteenth century, the gloss had grown to be the starting point for every exegesis of the *Clorpus Iuris*, and was even given force of law in some jurisdictions. The authority of the gloss is probably due to Accursius' very exhaustive coverage of Civil Law, in the course of which he not only pointed out its problems but also offered very wise solutions for them. Dictionnaire du Moyen Âge, sous la Direction de Claude Gauvard, Alain de Libera et Michel Ziruk, Quadrige, Puf, Paris, 2002, p. 592.
76. Bartolus wrote commentaries on all parts of the *Corpus Juris Civilis* (except *Justinian Institutes*), and also almost 400 legal opinions (*consilia*) written at the request of judges or private parties seeking legal advice.
77. *See* José Homem Correa Telles, Commentario crítico à Lei da Boa Razão em data de 18 de Agosto de 1769, Lisboa, 1865.

177. The main legislator of the *Code Napoléon*, the jurist Portalis, used to say that law was the law reduced into positive rules and particular perceptions, because it is created generically and does not aim to order a specific conduct but obliges everybody.

178. The former Brazilian Civil Code, published in 1916, was considerably inspired by these old laws. It was a patriarchal and individualist code in accordance with the Brazilian society at that time, but it allowed the opening of the law under certain circumstances, as described in the Introductory Law of Civil Code, Article 4: if the law presents a gap, the judge shall decide the case calling upon the analogy, the customs and the general principles of law.[78]

179. It is important to stress that the analogy, the equity, the general principles of law and the comparative law are not formal sources of law, but criteria for the integration of the legal rule.

180. The new Civil Code, published in 2002, maintained the past influences in some of its books, like the General Part of the Civil Code and the books on Family and Succession Law, but including profound changes in other parts of it, such as the Law of Obligations and Contract Law, and introducing new values, such as solidarity and functionality.

181. Concerning the special field of contract law, the sources are the Civil Code, customs and the general principles of law, as well as the fundamental principles of the Federal Constitution, which were also applicable to contracts (equality, non-discrimination, etc.).

182. Doctrine and jurisprudence are not considered primary sources in Brazil – except in family law – despite their great influence on court decisions.

183. Some aspects of Brazilian Contract Law have their sources in diverse and sparse laws like the Consumer Protection Code (*Código de Defesa do Consumidor*, Law n° 8.078 from 11 September 1990), and the Tenancy Law (*Lei do Inquilinato*, Law n° 8.245 from 18 October 1991, with changes by Law n° 12.112 from 9 December 2009).[79]

184. Nowadays, other kinds of rules and norms are imposed on nation states to make globalization possible. From that perspective, we can remark that numerous foreign rules are used in the juridical practice of various national systems. There are, for example, rules whose origin is the international or global instance, like the *Conduct Codes,* addressed to the public authority and even to private actors.

78. Lei de Introdução às normas do Direito Brasileiro Decreto-lei n° 4.657 from 4 Sep. 1942, drafting by law n° 12.376/2010.

79. For this matter, *see* Sérgio Pinto Martins, Instituições de Direito Público e Privado, 8th edition, São Paulo: Atlas, 2008, fls. 11–19.

185. Globalization poses a great number of challenges to Brazilian society, which has been obliged to update its communication tools and scientific apparatus to find new formulas to organize its national production system, to increase its productivity, to create new competitive standards and to work with new materials. In seeking to participate in the global society, Brazil has published new laws inspired by foreign rules and processes to avoid non-acceptance by the global society. One of the most important measures taken by the Brazilian government was to publish the new Anti-Corruption Law (*Lei Anticorrupção*, Law n° 12.846 from 2 August 2013 which came into force on 29 January 2014). Hence, the Brazilian government ratified the OECD Anti-Bribery Convention of 15 June 2000, which came into force by Decree 3.678 on 30 November 2000.[80]

186. The Brazilian government adopted the normative standards created by the Commissions or other organizations, like the Venice Commission concerning *l'État de Droit* and technical rules created by public or private organizations and networks, like the norms of the Bale Committee, related to banking and financial matters.[81] The Bale Agreement entered into force in Brazil on 1 October 2013. The International Organization for Standardization (ISO) Rules, the Associação Brasileira de Normas Técnicas (ABNT) Rules, Rules and Decisions of Internet Corporation for Assigned Names and Numbers (ICANN) (internet) and other rules concerning information and communication technology are examples of new norms that Brazil has adopted to meet the needs of globalization. On 23 April 2014, during the inauguration of the Encontro Multissetorial Global Sobre o Futuro da Governança da Internet (NET mundial) in São Paulo, the Brazilian president presented the Brazilian Civil Rights Framework for the Internet (*Marco Civil da Internet*).

187. Since that day, Brazil has had a legal framework to protect civil rights online.

188. Lastly, in this context, one question immediately comes to mind: Are all these norms sources of law? From our point of view, they are not. These norms are merely technical norms rather than legal rules. Nowadays, however, they play an important role, because due to the exchange between countries on different levels, a country such as Brazil must have the same efficient tools as more developed countries have in order to act on the commercial, technological and political scenes.

80. www.oecd.org/brazil.
81. Brazil adopted the Bale rules (II) in December 2004 by Communication n. 12.746.

Part I. General Principles of the Law of Contract

Chapter 1. Formation of a Contract

§1. Agreement a *Quid Pro Quo* (Reciprocity)

I. Offer and Acceptance

189. A consensual contract is formed when parties establish a legal relation between them.[82]

190. The first declaration is called an 'offer' (*proposta/oferta*) and the party who makes such a declaration is the 'offeror' (*proponente/policitante*). If the party who received the offer – the offeree (*aceitante/oblato*) – responds to it with another declaration indicating consent to its terms, such a declaration is called an 'acceptance' (*aceitação*).

191. Neither the offer nor the acceptance has the legal nature of a legal transaction (*negócio jurídico*). Offer and acceptance are pre-agreement actions directed towards defined or definable addressees with legal effects established by law.

192. In 'real contracts' or 'rights *in rem* contracts' (*contratos reais*), the conclusion of the agreement is subject to the actual transmission (*tradição*) of the object (*objeto* or rather *bem*) of the transaction.

193. Formal contracts (*contratos solenes*) are concluded only when their special forms, methods or conditions required by law are met.

194. More than one offeror and/or offeree may form a 'multiparty agreement' (*contrato plurilateral*). All parties to the agreement must declare acceptance to its terms, unless the declaration of all parties is not substantive to the conclusion of the agreement, as in insurance contracts.

82. Feiten Wingert Ody, Lisiane. *Direito e Arte*: O direito da arte brasileiro sistematizado a partir do paradigm alemão. São Paulo: Marcial Pons, 2018. p. 227.

195. The two phases of the formation of contracts – offer and acceptance – are analysed below.

II. Intent to Create Legal Relations

196. According to Orlando Gomes,[83] *the offer is the definite declaration of intent addressed to the person someone intends to conclude an agreement with, or to the public in general.*

197. The offer must contain all the essential elements of the proposed contract, so that the mere confirmation of its terms by the offeree is sufficient for the formation of the agreement. It must be *unequivocal, precise* and *complete*. The intention to contract is founded on the content of the declaration of will from the offeror.

198. Furthermore, it is necessary to distinguish an offer from an *invitation to treat* (*convite a fazer oferta*) – which is not an offer. However, it is admissible that an offer has some unspecified terms. For example, it is possible to leave the offeree to define the exact amount of goods that he or she intends to buy. The offer may also be addressed to an undefined but definable person, as is the case with public offers. Article 427 of the Brazilian Civil Code states, however, that the offer to contract obliges the offeror, unless the terms of the proposal, the nature of the trade or the circumstances of the case indicate otherwise.

199. According to Article 428 of the Brazilian Civil Code an offer ceases to be mandatory: when it is not immediately accepted, if a time for acceptance was not fixed; when it was not accepted after elapsing a sufficient length of time for a reply to have reached the offeror, if a time for acceptance was not fixed and the offer was made between absent parties; when a reply has not been issued before the expiration of the time fixed, if the offer was made between absent parties; or when the retraction of the offeror reaches the offeree before or by the same time he or she receives the offer.

200. Certain difficulties arise when it comes to the proof of an offer because it is hard to characterize all elements of a binding offer. It can be said, however, that the valid offer constitutes a potestative right for the offeree to conclude the agreement. According to A. Junqueira[84] this is particularly clear in regard to irrevocable or fixed-term offers. The retraction of the offer, in such cases, gives rise to liabilities of a contractual nature.

201. The obligation that emerges from the offer does not have the effect of binding the offeror to the proposed contract if its retraction occurs before the acceptance. The obligation is then converted to damages.

---

83. Contratos, Editora Forense, Rio de Janeiro, 12th edition, 1991, p. 65.
84. Junqueira De Azevedo, Antonio. A Boa Fé na formação dos contratos. In: Revista Direito do Consumidor nº 3, 1992, Editora Revista dos Tribunais, São Paulo, p. 83.

202. Acceptance is the *acquiescence to an offer*. The offeree integrates his or her will into the offeror's through an express declaration; the performance of actions that demonstrate his or her intention; or even by silence, in circumstances where he or she is required to express the intention but fails to do so.

203. Silence is only appropriate in certain situations. Generally, it does not amount to a declaration of intent, unless the law, the agreement between the parties or the applicable usages dictate otherwise.[85]

204. A declaration of acceptance has to come to the knowledge of the offeror in order to be effective: it is a directed declaration of will (*declaração receptícia de vontade*), representing the exercise of a (potestative) right of the acceptor, the right to conclude the agreement, the intent to contract.

205. In some cases, the acceptance is expressed through acts of performance, such as initiating the performance of the proposed agreement. Another example is 'qualified silence' (*silêncio circunstanciado*).

206. To conclude the contract, the intentions of both parties – offeror and acceptor – must match. If the intentions do not match, there is a dissent (*dissenso*) – a disagreement between the parties about essential aspects of the contract.

207. The offeree may also propose a counter-offer introducing modifications to the original terms. The contract is not formed and the previous situation is reversed. The offeree becomes the offeror. Nonetheless, a simple request for a price reduction from the offeree does not amount to a counter-offer.

208. It is also important to highlight that the place of the formation of the contract is of uttermost importance. The place of conclusion of the agreement determines the competent jurisdiction to rule over disputes arising from it and also, in the field of conflict of laws, it determines the law applicable to the contract.

209. If the contract was formed between absent parties, the place of conclusion is the place where the offer was issued. Contracts formed through the exchange of mail are considered to be formed between absent parties. Yet, contracts formed by phone are not considered contracts formed by absent parties and thus are regarded as formed where the offer was issued.

III. Offer and Acceptance in Adhesion Contracts

210. Adhesion contracts (*contratos de/por adesão*) constitute one of the most discussed and controversial issues of contract law. Such contracts are widely used to curb freedom of contract. With this technique, the content of the contract is translated into detailed provisions and the parties are limited to simply transcript such

85. C. A. da Mota Pinto, Teoria Geral do Direito Civil, Coimbra Editora, 1985, pp. 427 et seq.

provisions into contract clauses. The contract is then regulated as a whole, avoiding all kinds of preliminary discussions regarding its content. The most intriguing feature is that the contract is drawn up by only one of the parties, which, thus, normally would not be accepted as a genuine contract. Because of these characteristics, one of the parties will only be entitled to accept or reject the content of the contract previously established by the other party – hence the name *adhesion* contract.

211. Depending on the observer's perspective, the contractual relation will have different designations. From the perspective of the elaboration of contract terms by one of the parties, this relationship is called 'general business conditions' (or 'general contract conditions'). After the formation of the contract it is designated an 'adhesion contract' because it is then analysed from the perspective of its legal effectiveness (*eficácia*) as a bilateral legal relationship.

212. According to the renowned Civil Law professor from Spain, Garcia Amico, 'the overlapping of the two aspects, general conditions and adhesion, means that they represent two different logical and chronological moments of the same phenomena'.[86]

213. Another interesting feature is that the general conditions can be accepted or adhered to by an infinite number of contracting parties, without creating any relation between one contract and the previous ones.

214. As referred by German scholars, general conditions are of little relevance to the legal world until they circulate – until then, they are ordinary *Musterformulare* (model form) or a *Stück Papier* (piece of paper). Nevertheless, Brazilian case law and scholars, under evident French influence, use the expression *adhesion contract* more frequently than *general conditions*, which is more common in Portugal and Germany. Several authors consider both expressions synonymous, even though *adhesion contract* is narrower than *general conditions*.

IV. Consideration

215. The requirement of consideration is comparable to the French '*cause*', which is not present in Brazilian law.[87] In Brazil, the idea of cause is related to the

86. Condiciones Generales de los Contratos, Editorial Revista de Derecho Privado, Madrid, 1969.
87. In France, the theory of cause was really the product of a prolonged moral and philosophical preoccupation with human will which in law was allowed to produce effects only if it was externalised for an ascertainable and specific purpose. In bilateral contracts this could only be undertaken by the other party. Consideration, on the other hand, was devised by commercially minded lawyers at a time when they were anxious to escape from their formalistic medieval laws and expand their law of contracts. Through different routes, cause and consideration thus came to underline the interdependence of obligations of the contracting parties (Basil Markesinis, Foreign Law and Comparative Methodology: a subject and a Thesis, Hart Publishing, Oxford UK 1997, p. 47). France does not currently apply the concept of cause due to the European Union Law.

social-economic function of the contract, which means the aim of the contract. If the contract is used against that function it will be deemed null and void.[88]

A. Gratuitous Promises

216. Brazilian law admits gratuitous promises (*promessa de recompensa*) which generate obligations provided that the requirements are met: the person who, by public announcement, promises a reward or a bonus to whoever fulfils a certain condition or accomplishes a certain task, contracts the obligation to comply the promise (Article 854 CC/02). One important element of this unilateral act (*ato unilateral*) is the advertising or public expectation that the promise will be performed.[89]

217. The person who performs the service or fulfils the condition, even without any interest in the bonus, is entitled to demand the reward. If the act that is the object of the promise is performed by more than one person, the reward will be divided between them.

218. The law grants the promisor the right to withdraw the offer before the service is performed. Moreover, the promisor has to announce that he or she decided to withdraw the promise, in the same way he or she made the promise (Article 856 CC/02).

219. Promises made by public announcement need to include a deadline. This is an essential condition for the validity of the promise (Article 859 CC/02).

B. Natural Obligations

220. Natural obligations (*obrigação natural*) exist in the Brazilian legal system, as they do in German law. A natural obligation is not demandable, but once the debtor has performed it, it is impossible to change his or her mind and to reclaim any money. An example of a natural obligation in Brazilian law is the payment of a lapsed debt or of gambling debts.

V. Modifications to the Contract

221. A contract is subject to numerous circumstances; however, in principle, the rule of *pacta sunt servanda* should be observed.

88. *See* Orlando Gomes, Contratos, 12a edição, Forense, RJ, pp. 56–57; Judith Martins-Costa, A teoria da causa em perspectiva comparativista: a causa no sistema francês e no sistema civil brasileiro, Revista da Ajuris, v. 16, n. 45, março 1989, pp. 213–244.
89. *See* Part I, Chapter 6, § 8 (Restitution).

222. Roman law had admitted the possibility of a breach of contract – the breach of a promise would not always be unlawful, since a party would only be bound as long as such promise remained under the state's rule. Nonetheless, the Romans never formulated a specific rule in this regard. The Christian philosophers Augustine and Thomas Aquinas took up the same idea, developing a set of interesting theories that some of the most important European legal systems and European colonies would later adopt.

223. In this regard, Portugal adopted the clause *rebus sic stantibus*. It was present in the *Ordenações do Reino*, the legislation imposed on Brazil during the colonial period until the first Brazilian Civil Code of 1916 which largely preserved the content of the Portuguese legislation, since that law had been applied for almost three-hundred years.

224. With the large-scale codification movements of the nineteenth century, private autonomy was raised to the level of a supreme right. The stable economic conditions of that period supported this understanding. Hence, considering the will (*volonté*) as the supreme value, the maxim *qui dit contractuel, dit juste* (*what is contractual is fair*) was created. For this reason, nineteenth- and twentieth-century legislators refrained from inserting provisions to limit one's will in the codifications of that period.

225. Nevertheless, the two great wars triggered substantial modifications to contract law, giving rise to the *Theory of Unpredictability* (which incorporated a new component: the unpredictability of certain facts).

226. The difficulty of fulfilling contracts due to economic problems befallen after the formation of the contract, especially regarding long-term contracts, determined the evocation of the *rebus sic stantibus* clause. It was intended to attenuate the strictness of the *pacta sunt servanda* clause since some scholars argued that the contract's structure should be closely connected to the economic reality in order to provide stability in trade.[90]

227. Considering the close connection between the fulfilment of the contract and the prevailing economic conditions, the contract was not intangible.

228. Three main theories were developed to lessen the strictness of the old aphorism *pacta sunt servanda,* namely: the Theory of the Disappearance of the Contractual Basis (*Rompimento da Base do Negócio Jurídico*), arrived at from court decisions; the Theory of Imprevision (*Teoria da Imprevisão*) from France, originally related to public law; and Hardship (*Onerosidade Excessiva*) from Italy.

90. V. Clóvis do Couto e Silva, 'A teoria da Base do Negócio Jurídico' in: O Direito Privado brasileiro na visão de Clóvis do Couto e Silva. Fradera, Véra (org.). Porto Alegre, 2014, Livraria do Advogado, 2nd edition, pp. 87 et seq.

229. It is important to highlight the major role that the Principle of Objective Good Faith took in the development of the Disappearance of the Contractual Basis theory. The theory arose out of tension or polarization between the voluntarist aspects of the contract and the economic conditions that surrounded it, as explained in the classic work of Karl Larenz,[91] which was later taken up by Clóvis do Couto e Silva in several publications.

230. Article 317 of the Brazilian Civil Code from 2002 authorized the judicial review of contracts upon request of the damaged party in order to secure, as far as possible, the real value of the debt when a clear disproportion arises between the value of the debt and the time of its performance due to unforeseeable reasons.

231. Articles 478 et seq. refer to the possibility of terminating a continuing performance contract or deferred contract due to hardship – that is if the debt of one party becomes excessively onerous, with great benefit to the other party, because of extraordinary and unforeseeable events. The effects of the termination are retroactive to the date of service.

232. Analysing Article 317 of the Brazilian Civil Code, Professor Judith Martins-Costa stresses the relevance of distinguishing between the three theories. According to her, Brazilian case law applies the three theories indistinctly, based on the same *ratio*, while each theory has different requirements and effects. She states that when it comes to Article 317 of the Brazilian Civil Code the prevailing theory is the *Theory of Hardship*, despite the fact that the provision is intended to permit the review of contracts instead of their termination, as the Italian theory does. This understanding is based on the requirements of the Italian theory that are very similar to those prescribed in Article 317 of the Brazilian Civil Code. Judith Martins-Costa also states that Article 317 CC/02 does not serve as a basis for the application of the *Theory of Imprevision*, even though Brazilian case law has grounded the review of certain administrative contracts on such a theory. Although the provision refers to 'unpredictability' and 'clear disproportion', it makes no reference to the exceptionality of the event or to the extraordinary nature of the incident.[92]

§2. Formal and Evidential Requirements

I. Formal Requirements

233. There are no *contracts under seal* in the Brazilian legal system, since *consideration* does not constitute a legal requirement.

234. For *formal contracts* see the classification of contracts above (§2. Introduction to the Law of Contracts).

---

91. Geschäftsgrundlage und Vertragserfüllung, C.H. Beck, Berlin, 1957.
92. *See* Judith Martins – Costa. Comentários ao Novo Código Civil, Arts 304–388. vol. 1, editora Forense, Rio de Janeiro, 2005, pp. 278 et seq.

II. Evidential Requirements: Proof

A. *The Parol Evidence Rule*

235. According to Beviláqua,[93] evidence is the variety of measures used to lawfully demonstrate the existence of a juridical act.

236. Regarding the proof of contracts, Brazilian law has not adopted a rule similar to the parol evidence rule because the contract can be proven by any means, including documents, witnesses, assumptions, electronic files (regarded as documents under law), and public deeds. Testimonial evidence is only admitted to prove the existence of contracts whose value does not exceed ten times the current minimum wage in the country at the time of conclusion. Still, regardless of the value of the transaction, the Civil Code from 2002 admits oral evidence as a subsidiary or in addition to proof in writing (Article 227 and sole § CC/02).

237. The Civil Code and the Procedural Code regulate this matter.[94]

B. *Role of the Notary*

238. Brazil is a country of great contrasts when it comes to the distribution of wealth, climates, and also law, especially with regards to the relationship between public and private law. There are matters in which the state plays a significant role, such as consumer and family law, while it interferes only minimally in other areas, allowing the private sector as much freedom as possible.

239. In this sense, the current state of Brazilian private law corresponds to what Ludwig Raiser in the second half of the twentieth century in one of his speeches in a series of conferences in Brazil, which was called *The Future of Private Law* (published in the Journal of the Attorney General State of Rio Grande do Sul, nº 25, pp. 11 et seq.), described as a stepped structure of public and private interests. Examples are the possibility of separations and divorces, which today can be made before a notary instead of a judge, when there are no minor children and both parties have full capacity, or similarly, the drawing up of civil union contracts to establish the rules governing the couple's assets.

240. With regard to inventories and asset sharing, the notary is authorized to register them, provided there is no will and all the heirs are fully capable and agree on the destination of the shares of the deceased's estate. Interestingly, these notarial duties were already present in the Philippines Ordinances (First Book, title LXXVIII, 7) and suppressed in the Brazilian Civil Code of 1916. Despite the number of

93. Código Civil Comentado, vol. I, Editora Livraria Francisco Alves, 1959, Rio de Janeiro, pp. 129, 313.
94. *See* Clóvis do Couto e Silva, 'Direito Material e Processual em Matéria de Prova', Revista de Processo, vol. 13, São Paulo, Editora Revista dos Tribunais, January 1979, pp. 135–146.

duties assigned to notaries, there is no specific law in Brazil regulating this important activity. Brazilian notaries guide their activity by a few articles of the Civil Code and by customary norms, some of which have turned into standards as written by the judiciary and play an important role in monitoring the exercise of notarial activity as a result of constitutional powers (Article 236 CF/88) and Law n° 8.935/94. This particular piece of legislation establishes that notaries are not civil servants but rather public officers who exercise a delegated function; they are individuals who perform public services on their own behalf and at their own risk.

241. The field of contracts is an area with a large number of notarial acts, as, for example, the requirement of a public deed for the validity of legal transactions is aimed at the establishment, transfer, modification or waiver of rights in rem regarding real estate with a value which exceeds thirty times the highest minimum wage in the country.

242. The Brazilian legal system contains certain form requirements for certain transactions in order to protect each parties' declaration of will, which should be free and without defects, thus bringing greater security to the legal transactions. It is the notary's responsibility to protect such declarations of will and to contribute with his or her knowledge to the correction of the performed acts.

243. The notary and the notarial activity is one of the most important tools to guarantee legal certainty and control business relationships.

244. Currently, the role of notaries is gaining importance in the national legal universe. In addition, the small number of claims involving issues with notaries shows how well these services have been rendered.[95]

C. *Burden of Proof: Distinction Between Obligation of Means and Obligation of Results*

245. In Brazil, there is a distinction between obligations of means and of results (*obrigações de meio e obrigações de resultado*), a subject widely discussed in certain areas of civil law, for example, in the relationship between doctors and patients, regulated by the Consumer Protection Code.

246. In cases of civil liability for medical acts, there is still great controversy regarding the plastic surgeon's obligation, dividing doctrine and jurisprudence. While some understand this as an obligation of means, for the patient carries his or her idiosyncrasies (age, smoking or exposure to the sun, etc.), so that the result of a plastic surgery does not always depend only on the technique employed; others, erroneously in our view, consider that plastic surgery involves an obligation of results.

95. *See* Leonardo Brandelli, Teoria Geral do Direito Notarial, Editora Saraiva, São Paulo, 2007, 2nd edition.

247. However, there are obligations in the field of the medical profession that indeed are obligations of result, such as those of radiologists and haematologists.[96]

§3. Liability and Negotiations

I. Pre-contractual Liability

248. The legislator of the 2002 Civil Code did not consider the issue of pre-contractual liability; therefore, doctrine[97] and case law have been the main source of solutions to conflicts arising from abusive rupture of negotiations. Despite the occurrence of numerous cases of unjustified rupture of preliminary negotiations, there is no consensus on what the best solution for such cases should be.

249. However, it is interesting to note that among the legal systems in force in Latin America, the Brazilian system has some features, such as being divided according to the *Pandectas* and the legal theory regarding obligations, which distinguish it from the other systems. In addition the contribution from the *Pandectas*, the 2002 Civil Code has also been influenced by the *Josserand*[98] school, which gives a functionalist approach to the contract. Due to this particular perspective, both *pre-* and *post*-contractual agreements require a different treatment than that given to the same issues in systems inspired by the *Code Napoléon* in which a strong Canonist influence prevails.

250. Another notable aspect of Brazilian law is the fact that the legal relationship of an obligational nature is conceived as a process, in which the aim is the due performance. Therefore, parties should transpose successive stages composed of numerous duties of the most varied nature, collaborating instead of taking antagonistic positions, which is the case in systems dominated by the influence of French law. Cooperation between the parties due to the presence of *pandectism* is governed by principles, highlighting confidence and objective good faith.

251. Peculiarly, these principles have been applied and interpreted in Brazil in a similar manner to that of German courts. These principles have been widely applied and have been truly far-reaching since ancient times in the regions now forming Germany, e.g., in the courts of the Hanseatic League. They received their biggest

96. *See* Miguel Kfouri Neto, Responsabilidade Médica, Editora Revista dos Tribunais, São Paulo, 8th edition.
97. Judith Martins-Costa, Um aspecto da obrigação de indenizar: notas para uma sistematização dos deveres pré-negociais de proteção no direito civil brasileiro, in Estudos em Homenagem ao Professor Arnoldo Wald, A evolução do Direito no Século XXI, Almedina, Coimbra, 2007, pp. 301 et seq.; Cristiano de Sousa Zanetti, Responsabilidade pela Ruptura das Negociações, São Paulo, Editora Juarez de Oliveira, 2005; Carlyle Popp, Responsabilidade civil pré-negocial, Juruá Editora, Curitiba, 2001; Véra Jacob de Fradera, Dano Pré-contratual, uma análise comparativa a partir de três sistemas jurídicos: o continental europeu, o latino Americano e o Americano do norte, Revista de Informação Legislativa, vol. 34, nº 136, oct/dec., 1997, pp. 169–179.
98. For Josserand's doctrine *see* De l'Esprit des Droits et de leur Relativité, Dalloz, Paris, 2006.

boost following the German Coding, which was strongly marked by the principles of the Protestant Ethic. We will see that it is important to make this reference to German law, especially when we consider the specific design of the Law of Obligations as adopted in Brazilian law.

252. This issue will be addressed in two parts: first, we will present a cast of pre-contractual relationship forms admitted in legal transactions in general; then, we will present the ways in which Brazilian law intends to solve this problem.

A. *Forms of Pre-contractual Relationships Generally Admitted in Legal Transactions*

253. This issue is quite difficult, because the period prior to the contract consists of a set of facts without pre-established rules regarding the free negotiations based on the principle of private autonomy, a cornerstone of contract law. However, this area is widely described as being 'non-law' (from the French *non-droit*), a term coined by the sociologist and legal scholar Jean Carbonnier.

254. For other legal scholars, like Clóvis do Couto e Silva, the pre-contractual stage would be restricted to the grounds of the social contract, where the proximity between the parties is not as concrete as it is in a contract that has already been formed, but which, nevertheless, already requires behaviour guided by loyalty, trust, and, consequently, cooperation. It is the phase corresponding to the scope of the project in which the future contract is drawn up little by little in successive layers – *par couches successives.* These phases can have various denominations, for example, agreement in principle, *pourparlers*, punctuation, intent letter, memorandum of intent, engagement *d'honneur* or gentlemen's agreement, etc. with little or no difference between them. A common trait among them is the fact that the parties are negotiating a contract but have not entered into any yet. The contract may or may not occur depending on several factors.

255. Another point is that, today, the preliminary phase of the contract is crucial, especially if the contract fails to take shape despite there being negotiation. The parties might have come to an agreement in principle, assuming a possible turnaround when their performances are better defined or evaluated under specific terms and conditions. Thus, the ground is always shifting. The general agreement – whatever its name may be – may lead to a future acceptance, an acceptance subject to certain reservations or a refusal of the contract. As we can see, this field is characterized by total ambiguity contradicting the general outlines of private law.

256. When addressing this issue, one should mention the importance of the pre-contractual stage in international contracts, which differs from the understanding of national contracts. The prevailing practice among international negotiators is to avoid being bound until the last moment. As international trade negotiations are generally more extensive and durable and entail contracts involving large amounts of money, the damage resulting from failure to attribute responsibility for breaking the contract can be crucial.

257. We will now look into the solutions for these issues found in Brazilian law.

B. Reactions to Faulty Behaviour in the Pre-contractual Phase: Brazilian Solutions

258. As it is known, responses to violations in the phase prior to the birth of a contract rely on the notion of contract under the legal system in focus, and, above all, on the doctrinal, ethical and historical influences that mark its concepts. In this sense, we are aware of the distinct conceptions of contract in the *Code Napoléon* and the *BGB*. The former was drafted under individualistic and liberal inspiration, and, morally, in the light of Jansenism, while the latter is an artificial construction founded in *Pandectas* and dominated by a series of principles of which the most important is good faith. It is the basis of all structures drawn up by the Germans, a people of sellers, who, to make their trade attractive, endowed private law with numerous legal security mechanisms. With regards to morality, the BGB is predominantly characterized by principles of the Protestant ethic.

259. In the hypothesis of non-contractual or tortious liability, there may be no contract, but the parties would have contacted, discussed and negotiated, without, however, reaching a common denominator. In case that there is damage and fault is detected, there would be a causal relationship between the parties. The identification of simple fault, even without an intent to harm, characterizes the abuse of rights, in which the criterion is the notion of fault, which, alone, is not enough to impose the obligation to indemnify the exercise of a right where there has not been any damage. Thus, the exercise of a right entails liability; it is abusive when fault is established. Mistakenly, part of the national doctrine considers abusive conduct as involving strict liability, regardless of fault.[99]

260. On the other hand, the existence of a general obligation of good faith, required at the stage of formation of contracts,[100] should also govern the conduct of the parties during the negotiation phase, which may be terminated without a contract due to the exercise of the principle of private autonomy. However, it is not admissible to breach it after having raised the other party's confidence that a contract would be formed and such an attitude entails liability for loss.

261. Another point of support for the imposition of liability for abusive rupture of negotiations lies in the protection of trust, reflecting the need for security in legal transactions.

---

99. Declaration (Enunciado) 37 of the *I Jornada de Direito Civil.*

100. Article 422 CC. The contracting parties shall, at the conclusion of the contract as well as during their performance, adhere to the principles of Probity and Good Faith.

262. Obviously, the private law system stands on pillars: the first pillar consists of the principle of private autonomy, i.e., the expression of self-determination that is endowed upon every individual capable of actions under the law, who may establish, by will, legal effects recognized by law.

263. The second pillar is represented by the principle of mutual trust of social morality. It is the source of various duties among which the most important is that, in their contractual relationship, the parties must act in loyalty.

264. In Brazilian private law, many principles are inspired by German private law – the manifestations of the protection of good faith. Given the characteristics of this study, we will go into only two of these manifestations: *culpa in contrahendo* and the prohibition of the *venire contra factum proprium*, which can serve as a basis for accountability of those who violated the good faith of their counterparty, even in the pre-contractual stage.

II. Ihering's Discovery: The Notion of *Culpa in Contrahendo*

265. In 1861, Rudolf von Ihering formulated the theory of *culpa in contrahendo*, inspired by the spirit that guided the *Justinian's Corpus Juris* – the analysis of which allowed him to identify the thread linking invalid contracts, such as those in which the object is impossible, containing unilateral errors, involving revocation of the proposal before acceptance, and cases of supervening incapacity of the applicant. The apparently restricted scope under which the theory was conceived by von Ihering did not prevent it from being classified as a remarkable discovery, since it paved the way for further developments, which had never been previously considered.

266. Thus, the concept *culpa in contrahendo* came to be accepted as a general figure in the BGB system, thanks to the efforts of the Germanic doctrine and case law.

267. The discovery of von Ihering survived the coding of 1900 and the doctrine interpreted *culpa in contrahendo* in the light of the BGB, providing, shortly after its publication, elements for imposing a general obligation of correctness during negotiations.

268. As can be seen, one can apply duties under the principle of good faith, which guides contract law, to a non-contractual situation, for example, in the phase of negotiations, *pourparlers* or punctuations, and the liability arising therefrom is non-contractual given that the *culpa in contrahendo* derives from a particular kind of social contract, preceding the contract stage. Still, some authors claim it to be a contractual liability, even in the absence of a contract, because it entails different consequences from those which arise from tortious liability. Only as an example, we will quote Wolfgang Fikentscher who suggests that there is a 'common law' determining the application of contractual liability to cases of *culpa in contrahendo*. According to Couto e Silva, this is an artificial construction, reaffirming the nature of pre-contractual liability as tortious.[101]

269. Brazilian doctrine has affirmed that the undue disruption of negotiations must be sanctioned by applying *venire contra factum proprium*, which is also susceptible to various developments. This concept describes an act by the holder of a right that contradicts the conduct previously adopted, and upon which the counterparty had relied. According to this understanding, the fact that someone gives the impression that he or she would act in a way as to enter into an agreement, and, suddenly, for no real reason, put an end to negotiations, would configure a situation of *venire contra factum proprium*, breaching the principle of good faith in the objective sense.

270. Generally, Brazilian doctrine and case law allow for the attribution of responsibility for the breakdown of negotiations, based on the principle of good faith, if by the time of that breakdown the other party had been given reasons to assume a certain degree of confidence, and thus believed that the contract would be signed.

271. As it turns out, the rule on which the regulation of the pre-contractual stage rests is the principle of good faith, which relates to other principles connected to the pre-contractual and contractual phases, such as objective good faith and the prohibition of *venire contra factum proprium*.

272. Establishing a model of the pre-contractual duties of good faith arising from trade usage would be rather difficult, because although legal trading is similar everywhere, it is not easy to list parameters for general behaviour. Given this circumstance, the renowned German author Hildebrandt[102] systematized a series of pre-contractual duties including duties of disclosure (duty to inform exactly on the essential facts for the formation of contractual intent of the other party) and the duty of truth, which entails refraining from imprecise statements or propositions regarding key facts. These duties have been defined by the national doctrine as being required at the stage of negotiations preceding the formation a contract.

III. Conclusion

273. One key point is that party autonomy, viewed as an expression of the self-determination of individuals, is used voluntarily in relations, while good faith – the relevant element in the security of legal transactions – requires a sense of personal responsibility, whose legal consequences arise *ex lege* and not *ex voluntate*.

101. Fikentscher, Wolfgang. Schuldrecht, Berlin, Editor Walter de Gruyter, 1985, par. 20, II, 4, p. 66.
102. Hildebrandt *apud* Mário Júlio de Almeida Costa, Direito das Obrigações, 6. ed. Almedina, Coimbra, 1994, p. 246, note 2.

Chapter 2. Conditions of Substantive Validity

§1. Capacity of the Parties

274. According to Article 1 of the Civil Code, every person is capable of exercising rights and duties in the civil order. Legal personality (*personalidade jurídica*) is acquired at live birth by the functioning of the cardio-respiratory system (Resolution no. 1/88 of the National Health Council). In accordance with Article 2, the unborn child's rights (conceived, but not yet born) are safeguarded by the law since the child's conception.

275. According to the *Natalist Theory*, which is classic in Brazil (as per Eduardo Espínola, Vicente Rau, Sílvio Venosa, Sílvio Rodrigues, etc.), the unborn child is not considered a person, enjoying mere expectation of rights, since legal personality is only acquired at birth. The *Conceptionist Theory* (as per Teixeira de Freitas, Clóvis Beviláqua, Silmara Chinelato, etc.) also influences the Code because it recognizes rights of the unborn child such as the right to life, including protection against abortion, the right to prenatal protection, the right to receive gifts and inheritance, the right to have a curator appointed for his or her interests (Articles 877 and 878 CC/02), and the right to food during pregnancy (Law nº 11.804/2008, which regulates the pension for the pregnant mother).

276. Legal capacity (*capacidade civil*) is acquired together with legal personality, while legal incapacity may be absolute or relative. Those absolutely incapable of personally exercising the acts of civil life (*absolutamente incapazes*) are minors under sixteen years (Article 3 CC/02). Those relatively incapable (*relativamente incapazes*), for certain acts, or to the manner in which they are exercised, are minors over 16 and under 18 years, habitual drinkers and addicts of toxic substances and those who, even for a temporary cause, cannot express their will, as well as the prodigal. The capacity of native Brazilians is governed by special legislation (Article 4 CC/02).

277. Absolutely incapable persons must be represented, while relatively incapable people need a guardian. Relative incapacity reduces the capacity of discernment. If drunkenness is complete and pathological, it is a cause of incapacity. The prodigal, when relatively incapable, are interdicted and a curator is appointed to assist in acts of patrimonial nature. In Article 8, the Statute of Native Brazilians (Law nº 6.001/73) generally considers native Brazilians who do not display awareness of practised actions to be absolutely incapable.

278. In general, as per Article 5 CC/02, minority ceases at the age of 18, when the person is empowered to perform all acts of civil life. In turn, emancipation (*emancipação*) is a form of anticipation of full capacity. It may be voluntary, judicial or legal. Incapacity of minors ceases when granted by both parents, or one parent in the absence of the other, through a public instrument, regardless of judicial approval or by decision of a judge after hearing the guardian, if the minor is 16 years old; by marriage; by the effective exercise of public employment; by graduation from a higher education course; and by the foundation of a civil or commercial establishment, or the existence of an employment relationship, provided that, because of such, the minor is economically independent (Article 5 CC/02).

279. Emancipation is not a typical concept of Brazilian law, but rather found in other countries such as Switzerland, Germany, Portugal, etc. Portugal had particular influence, as per Article 133 of the Portuguese Civil Code: emancipation, grants full capacity for the exercise of rights to minors, enabling them to fully govern their rights and assets.

280. The death of an individual occurs when a person is brain dead, which is considered as a safer reference for the moment of death, including for transplant purposes (Resolution no. 1.480/97 of the Federal Council of Medicine). Death must be certified by a medical professional, but, in the absence of a specialist, it may also be declared by two witnesses.

281. There is the presumptive death hypothesis due to absence (*morte presumida pela ausência*, Article 6 CC/02), when a person disappears from his or her home without giving notice or leaving a representative to manage his or her assets. The procedure is regulated by Article 22 CC/02 concerning the curator of the assets, as well as the provisional and final succession. When the judge opens the final succession for the missing person's assets, he or she is declared dead by presumption.

282. There is also the presumptive death without declaration of absence (*morte presumida sem declaração de ausência*, Article 7 CC/02). When the death of a person who was in danger of life or who was missing during war or taken as prisoner and not found until two years after the end of the war, is extremely likely, the judge gathers evidence and makes a decision declaring the death, which must be recorded in the registry of deaths. The decision must fix the alleged date of death. If a person who was presumed dead returns, he or she must initiate the necessary proceedings in order to declare the nullity of the act which declared him or her dead.

283. The Brazilian Civil Code refers to simultaneous death, when it is not possible to establish the chronological order of death between two or more people (*comoriência*). The Brazilian Civil Code has not adopted a listing of assumptions as the French code has. If it is not possible to specify the order of death, it is assumed that all persons died simultaneously, opening autonomous and distinct succession chains.[103]

---

103. *See* the recent article from Henrique Rabelo Quirino, Considerações críticas sobre a presunção de comoriência, Rev.do Centro Acadêmico Afonso Pena CAAP, Belo Horizonte, n. 1, vol. XXIV, p. 108, 2019.

§2. DEFECTS OF CONSENT

284. The list of legal transaction defects in Brazil is not limited to the defects in consent (*vício de consentimento*) and also provides for *laesio enormis* (*lesão*) and fraud against creditors (*fraude a credores*).

I. Error (Distinction from Value; Distinction from Motive)/ Misrepresentation and Deceit

285. Article 138 of the Civil Code contains the list of transaction defects arising from error (*erro*) or ignorance (*ignorância*) and states that legal transactions are voidable when declarations of consent are issued based on substantial errors that could be perceived by a person of reasonable diligence according to the business circumstances.

286. Theoretically, an error[104] is a false perception of reality, an uninduced misinterpretation of a situation. Ignorance, in turn, is a state of lack of knowledge. The consequence of both error and ignorance is the possible invalidity of the transaction.

287. However, not all errors lead to the annulment of the transaction. The classical doctrine, since Clovis Beviláqua, stated that for the error to be a disabling cause of the transaction it should be essential and excusable. The current doctrine, interpreting Article 138 CC/02, deems the excusability of the error to be irrelevant for the invalidation of the transaction. The classical thought is therefore criticized with regard to the principle of good faith, according to which the person who was wrong relied on the other party (to judge whether this is forgivable or not is very subjective).

288. Article 139 CC/02 describes three basic forms of error: First, an error is substantial when it affects the nature of the transaction, the main object of the statement or any of its essential qualities. Second, there is a substantial error when it is the only or main reason for the transaction, while being legal and not implying refusal to apply the law. It focuses on the structure of the transaction's declarations of will. Lastly, any error concerning the identity or the essential nature of the person to whom the declaration of intention is addressed is substantial, provided that it has influenced that declaration to a significant degree. This type of error is linked to the personal characteristics of the declarant, which has particular application in family law for marriage annulment effects, because the marriage can be voided due to defects of consent, if one of the spouses was in essential error as to the other person (Articles 1.556 and 1.557 CC/02).

104. On this matter, *see* Caio Mário da Silva Pereira, Introdução ao Direito Civil, Forense, Rio de Janeiro, 1965, pp. 389 et seq.

289. Traditionally, according to the teaching of Clovis Beviláqua and, along the same lines, the 1916 Civil Code, the thesis that an error of law could invalidate a legal transaction was not admissible. Later, authors like Eduardo Espínola, Carvalho Santos and Caio Mário supported this possibility, since it does not translate intentional refusal to the application of law. The 2002 Civil Code, in Article 139 III, admits error of law as a cause of invalidity of the transaction given that the agent interprets the law wrongly. Thus, an error of law is justified where the declarant in good faith is mistaken as to the scope of permissive action of the rule. This is a possible error which occurs regarding the illegality of facts.

290. The error (which meets the criteria referred to above) is a cause of invalidity of the transaction and leads to its annulment. However, it is worth noting that, pursuant to Article 144 CC/02, the error does not invalidate the transaction if the loss is restored. It does not affect the validity of the transaction when the person to whom the declaration of intent is addressed offers to execute it in accordance with the real intention of the party.[105]

291. The second defect referred to in the Civil Code is deceit (*dolo*), which can candidly be defined as intentional error, which results in the invalidity of the transaction (annulment). Deceit is intentionally caused and implies cunning (unlike the error, which is spontaneous). Although both error and deceit may cause a transaction to be voided, on an axiological and evaluative scale, deceit is more detestable and reprehensible than error.

292. In contract law theory, as *per* Article 145 CC/02, intentional deceit must be the central cause of a legal transaction in order to make it voidable due to fraud. By contrast, in the case of where the deceit does not affect the validity of the contract, thus imposing only an obligation to pay damages, it is called *dolo acidental*. Deceit is considered accidental when, despite the deceit, the contract is concluded, although in another way (Article 146 CC/02). Accidental deceit is secondary and does not preclude the parties from maintaining the contract.

293. Negative deceit (*dolo por omissão; dolo negative*), in turn, is even more serious than positive deceit, consisting in the breach of the principle of good faith by failure of the duty to inform, as per the omission of essential information concerning the fact or quality that the other party may have ignored at the time of the transaction is concluded. Intentional silence of a party constitutes malicious omission, provided that there is proof that without it the transaction would not have been concluded (Article 147 CC/02). To inform is one of the ancillary duties or protection duties imposed by the objective food faith (Article 422 CC/02).

294. In addition, there is mutual deceit (*dolo recíproco*). In Brazil, there is a popular saying according to which '*a thief who steals from a thief has one hundred*

105. *See* Carlos Nelson Konder, Erro, Dolo e Coação: Autonomia e Confiança na celebração dos negócios jurídicos, in Manual de Teoria Geral do Direito Civil, (orgs.) Ana Carolina Brochado Teixeira e Gustavo Pereira Leite Ribeiro, Editora Del Rey, Belo Horizonte, 2011, p. 633.

years of forgiveness'. Article 150 CC/02 provides that, upon mutual (bilateral) deceit – that is, when the two parties intended to deceive each other – the legal transaction shall remain as it is, and neither party is allowed to claim damages. This does not imply a 'compensation' for deceit, but the transaction is left for the parties to bear their own turpitude.

295. Regarding third-party deceit (*dolo de terceiro*), a deal is cancelled only if the party who benefited from the transaction knew or ought to have known the intent (if there was collusion between the party who benefited and the third party). If the beneficiary of the deceit did not know and had no way of knowing about the deceit of the third party, there is no cancellation of the deal, but only an undertaking by the third party to indemnify any damages.

296. In other words, according to Article 148 CC/02, deceit by a third party only invalidates the legal transaction if its beneficiary knew or ought to have known about it. Otherwise, if the beneficiary did not know nor ought to have known, the transaction is maintained and the third party can be held liable for all losses and damages suffered by whomever he or she deceived.

II. Improper Pressure

297. Coercion (*coação*), in order to taint a declaration of consent, must instil in the victim a founded fear of imminent and considerable harm to the person, family or property. It includes any psychological violence employed to influence the victim to perform a legal transaction that the victim by his/her internal will would not want to make. If it concerns a person who does not belong to the victim's family, the judge, based on the circumstances, shall decide whether there was coercion (Article 151 CC/02).

298. According to Article 152 CC/02, coercion should always be assessed concretely and never abstractly. Aspects such as gender, age, condition, health, the victim's temperament and all other circumstances that may influence its severity must be taken into account.

299. One must not confuse psychological coercion with physical coercion, which renders the legal transaction non-existent. Coercion, as it is treated in this essay, constitutes grounds for invalidity of a transaction. Also, one must not confuse coercion with the threat of regular exercise of a right or a simple dread in the absence of an actual threat (Article 153 CC/02). Dread is respect for an established authority (possibly in one's family, professional, ecclesiastical, or military circle, etc.).

300. Unlike what happens in the case of deceit by a third party, in the case of coercion by a third party, such party is to be held jointly liable for damages with the benefiting party and the legal action is defective if the benefiting party knew or ought to have known about the coercion (Article 154 CC/02). The legal transaction is upheld provided that the party who benefited from a third party's coercion did not know nor had any means of knowing about the coercion. The third party, however, is liable for all damages caused (Article 155 CC/02).[106]

301. In the case of fraud, if there are any claims for damages after the annulment of the contract, the benefiting party and the third party shall be held individually liable for damages to the extent of their guilt.

III. Gross Disparity

302. *Laesio enormis* (*lesão*) is the transactional flaw which is closest to the 'abuse of economic power'. The 1916 Civil Code did not address the issue, which has its roots in Roman law.

303. In Brazil, the first analysis of the issue of *leasio enormis* and usury (*usura*) was undertaken not in civil but in criminal law: it was Law nº 1.521/51 (Popular Economy Law, *Lei de Crimes contra a Economia Popular*), which established the crime of 'usury in contracts'. In the field of private law, the first great law which governed the matter was the Consumer Protection Code, which refers to *laesio enormis* more than once, always grounded on Article 6 V of this code which states that among the basic consumer rights is the modification of contractual clauses establishing disproportionate instalments, or revision in view of subsequent events that render the contract too onerous.

304. Article 157 of the 2002 Civil Code extended the application of *laesio enormis* beyond business and consumer relations, defining that it occurs when a person, due to an urgent need or inexperience, assumes an obligation constituting a manifestly disproportionate benefit to the value of the opposite provision. The disproportion of benefits must be assessed according to the values applicable at the time of conclusion of the transaction. Furthermore, the transaction shall not be voided if it offered sufficient supplement or if the party who benefited agrees to reduce the advantage.

305. Nowadays, *laesio enormis*/usury is one of the main reasons for applications to review bank contracts regarding interest rates. However, such cases rarely succeed before Brazilian higher courts, because it is understood that financial institutions are not restricted to interest limitations as per the Usury Act.

306. A defect of consent caused by *laesio enormis* is closely connected to the abuse of economic power and renders the transaction invalid. Such a defect becomes evident in the disparity between the benefits of the transaction (one party's obligations are excessive compared to the other's) due to the abuse in the face of

106. Carlos Nelson Konder, Erro, Dolo e Coação: Autonomia e Confiança na celebração dos negócios jurídicos, in Manual de Teoria Geral do Direito Civil, (orgs.) Ana Carolina Brochado Teixeira e Gustavo Pereira Leite Ribeiro, Editora DelRey, Belo Horizonte, 2011, p. 609.

need or inexperience of one of the parties. The impaired party does not necessarily need to be poor. A rich person who has a pressing need for resources or is inexperienced could suffer under such a defect. Generally, however, *laesio enormis* more often affects those who are hypo-sufficient.[107]

307. *Laesio enormis* is composed of two elements: First, the material or objective element, i.e., a disproportion between the transaction's benefits. The Civil Code provides an open concept for the judge without establishing a mathematical criterion to say what characterizes the disproportion (it does not state, e.g., that there is *laesio enormis* when the value of the benefit is three times higher than the market value). Second, the intangible or subjective element, i.e. the need or inexperience of the party who undertakes the excessive obligation.

308. Unlike some European countries, such as Italy and Germany, Brazil exempts the traditional third element, the *abuse* (intention of the party who benefits to take advantage of the other party), making it easier for the injured party to demonstrate the occurrence of the *laesio enormis*.

309. Within the scope of civil law (civil affairs in general), *laesio enormis* is a cause for annulment of a transaction, according to Article 157 CC/02. However, under the scope of consumer law, given its principles of public policy, it is a basis for absolute nullity of the transaction.

310. State of danger (*estado de perigo*), in turn, appears when someone in a situation of severe risk of damage and pressed by the need to save one's self or one's family member from serious injury, of which the other party is aware, assumes an excessively onerous obligation. If the threat is to a person other than a family member, the judge shall decide according to the circumstances (Article 156 CC/02).

311. Some say that in the 'state of danger', there is a kind of exploitation of intent since the other party is aware of the danger.

312. Unlike *laesio enormis*, the state of danger of a party is built on a situation of total desperation with imminent danger of harm to health, life, physical and moral integrity, etc. It also gives grounds to void the transaction.

107. Rodolfo Barreto Sampaio Junior, Estado de Perigo e Lesão, in Manual de Teoria Geral do Direito Civil, Ana Carolina Brochado Teixeira e Gustavo Pereira Leite Ribeiro (orgs.), Editora Del Rey, Belo Horizonte, 2011, p. 633.

§3. Other Conditions of Validity

I. Existing and Licit Object

313. A legal transaction should be analysed on three levels, not in the order of prevalence, but in that of logical precedence, namely: the existence level, the validity level and the effectiveness level, examining the conditions for the existence of the transaction (expression of consent, agent, object and form) and its validity requirements (capable agent, licit, possible, determined or determinable object and form as prescribed or not forbidden by law, as referred to in Article 104 CC/02).

314. On the existence level, one must analyse the conditions for the existence or constituent elements of the transaction, without which the legal transaction does not exist.

315. As per Article 111 CC/02, in line with Article 218 of the Portuguese Code (and of other countries such as Belgium, Germany, etc.), silence can generate legal effects when circumstances or uses permit it and the express declaration of consent is not required;[108] e.g., in pure donations, the silence of the party receiving the donation within the prescribed period means acquiescence (Article 539 CC/02[109]). Therefore, in some situations, silence is consent.

316. Silence is of great importance in situations of negative deceit. As referred to above, Article 147 CC/02 states that in bilateral legal transactions, intentional silence of a party concerning facts or qualities that the other party may have ignored constitutes malicious omission, provided there is proof that without it the transaction would not have been concluded.

317. The validity requirements translate into qualification requirements for the transaction to generate legal effects. The validity requirements are built on the existence requirements, which are qualified as the following:

Existence Requirements	*Validity Requirements*
Declaration of intent	*Free* declaration of intent in accordance with *good faith*
Agent	*Capable* and *legitimized* agent

108. On this matter, *see* Priscila Sansone Tutikian, O silêncio na formação dos contratos, Livraria do Advogado Editora, Porto Alegre, 2009; Vera Jacob de Fradera, O valor do silêncio no novo Código Civil, in Aspectos Controvertidos do novo Código Civil, Editora Revista dos Tribunais, São Paulo, 2003.

109. Article 539 CC. The donor may specify the time within which the recipient must declare whether or not he or she accepts the donation. If the recipient is aware of this term and does not respond to the donation within such term, the donations is considered accepted, if the gifts are not subject to charge.

Existence Requirements	*Validity Requirements*
Object	*Lawful*, *possible* and *determined* or *determinable* object
Form	*Free* or *prescribed by law*

II. Determined or Determinable, Possible and Licit Object or a Lack of Substantive Validity

318. The object must be lawful, possible, determined or determinable. Lawfulness, according to Orlando Gomes,[110] translates to compatibility with the law and with the average standard of morality. In Brazil, the legal culture has not firmly established an average standard of morality and customs, but simple compatibility with the law is understood to be insufficient.

319. Regarding form, Article 107 CC/02 enshrines the principle of freedom of form as a general rule. By exception, however, the law may require a certain form and thus a public deed for the following purposes: to serve as evidence of the transaction (Article 227 CC/02[111]), which is referred to as *ad probationem*; or to provide the validity of transactions which aim to establish, transfer, modify or waive real estate property worth more than thirty times the highest minimum wage in the country (Article 108 CC/02), which is referred to as *ad solemnitatem*.

320. Failure to comply with the legally required form prevents parties from proving a determined transaction. Failure to comply with the legally required form for validity renders the transaction invalid. As for the minimum wage, for the purpose of application of the articles referred to above, as a rule, the national minimum wage is used (in Brazil there are also regional minimum wages).

321. Also, it is important to note that under the exception of the first part of Article 108 CC/02 ('unless otherwise specified by law'), the non-compliance with the public form is admitted through exception provided for by the law, even in transactions related to real estate property and even if the value dealt with in the transaction exceeds thirty times the minimum wage; e.g., a purchase and sale promise (Articles 1.417[112] and 1.418 CC/02[113]).

110. Introdução ao Direito Civil, Editora Forense, Rio de Janeiro, 1965, 2ª edição, pp. 175 et seq.

111. Article 227 CC. Except for the expressed cases, evidence constituted exclusively of witness statements are only admitted in legal transactions whose value does not exceed ten times the minimum wage in the country at the time they were concluded. Paragraph. Whatever the value of the transaction may be, witness statements are admissible as subsidiary or additional proof in writing.

112. Article 1.417 CC. A purchase and sale promise without any right of repentance, whether celebrated by public or private instrument and recorded in the Registry of Deeds, shall provide the prospective buyer with the right to purchase the property.

III. Initial Impossibility

322. See *laesio enormis,* in Part I. General Principles of the Law of Contract, Chapter 2, § 2º Defects of consent, section III. Gross Disparity.

§4. The Consequences of a Defect of Consent or a Lack of Substantive Validity

I. Avoidance of the Contract: Nullity

323. Invalidity (*invalidade*) includes both absolute nullity and relative nullity (possibility of annulment). Some systems treat the invalid act as an illicit act. In Brazil, it is an independent category.[114]

324. On an axiological scale, absolute nullity is more serious than relative nullity, since absolute nullity violates rules of public policy, i.e., mandatory rules, while the relative nullity (possibility of annulment) violates merely operative rules, which protect private interests.

325. In the analysis of invalidity, respect for the principle of preservation should be ensured. That is, whenever possible, the judge should try to save an invalid transaction. Considering the intent of the parties, the partial invalidity of a transaction shall not harm its valid parts, if it is separable. The invalidity of the main obligation causes the invalidity of the ancillary obligations; but not vice versa (Article 184 CC/02).

326. Every nullity presupposes a rule that declares it. The parties cannot create new nullities. It is an issue of legal predictability.

327. Absolute nullities (*nulidade absoluta*) are governed by Articles 166–167 CC/02. These state that the legal transaction is null when I – it is celebrated by persons who are absolutely incapable; II – it is unlawful, impossible or has an indeterminable object; III – the decisive reason, common to both parties, is unlawful; IV – it does not take the form prescribed by law; V – it lacks the solemnity the law considers essential for its validity; VI – it is intended to infringe mandatory law; or VII – the law flatly declares it null or prohibits its practice without establishing a penalty (Article 166 CC/02). A simulated legal transaction is also null but what was concealed shall stand, if it is valid in substance and form. It is considered simulated

113. Article 1.418 CC. The prospective buyer, the holder of the right to purchase the property, may require the prospective seller or third parties to whom the rights are transferred to, to grant the final deed of sale, pursuant to the preliminary instrument; and if there is refusal, he or she may request before a judge to receive the property's deed.

114. For the most relevant aspects of this matter, *see* Marcos Bernardes de Mello, Teoria do Fato Jurídico, Plano da Existência, Editora Saraiva, São Paulo, 13th edition, 2007; by the same author, Teoria do Fato Jurídico, Plano da Validade, Editora Saraiva, São Paulo, 7th edition, 2006 and Teoria do Fato Jurídico, Plano da Eficácia, 1st part, 3rd edition, 2007.

when it appears to confer or transfer rights to persons other than those to which they actually confer or transfer, when it contains statements, confessions, conditions or clauses which are untrue or when the particular instruments are backdated or post-dated. The rights of third parties in good faith shall be upheld against contracting parties in a simulated legal transaction (Article 167 CC/02).

328. Due to its severity, absolute nullity may be claimed by anyone, including the state's counsel (when intervening in the procedure), or can be recognized directly by the judge when he or she analyses the legal transaction or its effects and finds proof of such nullities. It is not permitted to overcome them, even in the face of request by the parties (Article 168 CC/02).

II. Retroactive Effect of Avoidance or Nullity

329. Absolute nullities do not allow confirmation nor do they convalesce over time (Article 169 CC/02).

330. A declaratory ruling of absolute nullity produces *ex tunc* effects (retroactive), safeguarding third parties in good faith.

III. Relative Nullity or Possibility of Annulment of the Transaction

331. Relative nullity (*nulidade relativa*) is less severe because it affronts operative rules. A legal transaction can be voided due to relative incapacity of the agent or due to defects resulting from errors, deceit, coercion, state of danger, *laesio enormis* or fraud against creditors (Article 171 CC/02).

332. However, Article 171 CC/02 does not exhaust all the possibilities of relative nullity, as the first part of the provision states. The Civil Code provides other possibilities of relative nullity – e.g., Article 496 CC,[115] the possibility of voiding a purchase and sale to one's descendant without hearing the other descendants.

333. A possibly void legal transaction can only be challenged within the legal deadlines and by those with legitimate legal interest and it shall only benefit the parties which have claimed it, except in the case of solidarity (joint and several liability) or indivisibility. Economic or moral interest is not sufficient (Article 177 CC/02). The limitation period to plead the annulment of a transaction is of four years. In the case of coercion, this period starts on the day on which it ceases, in case of error, deceit, fraud against creditors, state of danger or *laesio enormis*, on the day on which the legal transaction was performed and in the case of acts by incapable persons, on the day of the termination of the incapacity (Article 178 CC/02).

115. Article 496 CC. The sale of ascendant to descendant is voidable, unless the remaining descendants and the transferor's spouse have expressly consented. Sole §. In both cases, the spousal consent is exempted if the property regime is mandatory separation.

When the law provides that a certain act is subject to annulment, without establishing a term to plead such annulment, this term shall be of two years from the date of completion of the act (Article 179 CC/02). Thus, the annulment does not expire.

334. Unlike null transactions, voidable transactions admit express or implied confirmation because they are less severe.

335. A voidable contract generates effects until a judge declares it void (with *ex tunc* effectiveness). When a contract is voided, the parties shall restore the state they were in before, and, if that is not possible, they shall be indemnified in the equivalent amount (Article 182 CC/02).

336. Inspired by the *BGB,* the consolidation of a voidable contract is admitted as a remedy in the Brazilian Civil code. If a contract deemed null and void has the elements of another valid contract, these shall be deemed to be valid, if it is considered the parties would have wanted that if they had foreseen the nullity (Article 170 CC/02). Through this remedy, the parties use the material elements of a null or voidable transaction, turning it into another lawful transaction.[116]

IV. Damages

337. As a consequence of the nullity or annulment of the legal transaction, the reparation of damages (*reparação dos danos*) by the defaulting party is admitted both before State courts and arbitration tribunals.

338. The reparation of civil damages includes direct damages, lost profits, as well as interest, an update of the monetary values and legal fees (Articles 395 and 402 CC/02).

116. Carlos Roberto Barbosa Moreira, Conversão do Negócio Jurídico, in Manual de Teoria Geral do Direito Civil, (orgs.) Ana Carolina Brochado Teixeira e Gustavo Pereira Leite Ribeiro Editora Del-Rey, Belo Horizonte, 2011, p. 677.

Chapter 3. Contents of a Contract

§1. Different Clauses

I. Ascertaining Express Terms

339. A contract can be formed in different manners, because the consent is exteriorized by declarations, expressed in distinct forms or aspects. Thus, the declaration can be verbal, written or symbolic.

340. A declaration is verbal when it is expressed in words, addressed to a person, with whom the declaring person wants to contract. This form of declaration can be done by telephone, fax, or an electronic message (e-mail).

341. A declaration is written when its content is expressed in a document, manuscript, typed or digitalized and signed by the declarant.

342. These considerations have the purpose of introducing the subject referred to in Chapter 3, about the contract's standard terms.

343. Normally, the contract takes the form of a set of dispositions, which covers the contents of it, i.e., the way a certain contract will be structured, taking into account the interests of the respective parties.

344. The contract can be redacted in the way that pleases the parties, but a written contract contains a preamble and a set of clauses, which depending on their importance are classified as being either essential, natural or accidental clauses (*elementos essenciais, naturais or acidentais*).

345. As the word 'essential' suggests, these clauses, such as those indicating the price of the object or the purpose of the contract, must be necessarily written into the contract.

346. Natural clauses, such as the prevision of a guarantee of the contract, or the guarantee against eviction in contracts transferring goods are foreseen in the law, but their introduction in the contract is not mandatory.

347. Accidental clauses are written in the contract, when the parties want to subordinate their efficacy to a future event that is uncertain.

348. Expressed clauses are written in the contract on the agreement of the parties, taking their private interests into account.

II. Implied Terms

349. Implied clauses (*cláusulas implícitas*) do not need to be expressed in the contract. In the Brazilian Civil Code, Article 113 states that some clauses must be considered as agreed by the parties, considering their precedent relationships, the customs of the commercial branch, the local customs and the circumstances. Article 478 CC/02[117] governs that, in the same way, the annexed duties and those deduced from the principle of good faith must be observed by the parties, even if they are not expressed in writing. Another notable implied clause is in Article 474 CC/02[118] which states that in bilateral contracts, if one of the parties fails to perform his or her obligation, the contract is dissolved. Only implied clauses require a judge's consent.

350. Incidentally, the Consumer Protection Code refers to a quality duty, i.e., an annexed duty, which is addressed to the suppliers as an implied guarantee and consists of the duty to offer products without defects. According to the Brazilian doctrine, these guarantees, despite their origin in the implied warranties of the common law, are wider, because they cannot be limited by the contractual guarantee, because of their special nature, *ex lege.*[119]

III. Standard Terms and Exemption Clauses

351. *Standard terms* are frequently employed in Brazilian contractual law, under the denomination of *standard contracts* (*contrato-padrão*), which, regarding their form, are very similar to adhesion contracts. In the functional aspect, a standard contract is employed when the future partners belong to opposite organized categories of interested parties. The structure of standard contracts is very often decided by both contracting parties.

352. Commonly, the interested parties organize their relationships under standard contracts, which allow them to define the essential elements of their agreements, without the obligation to establish concrete modalities. The essential obligation of these contracts consists of concluding contracts grounded on the requests exchanged by the parties. These standard contracts are, for example, the basis of contracts regarding integrated distribution systems, i.e., exclusive, concession distribution and selective distribution contracts (in which there is a limitation to the number of resellers, by wholesale or retail) and to franchise contracts.

117. Article 478 CC. In contracts with continuous or deferred performance, the debtor may request the termination of the contract, if the debt of one party becomes excessively onerous with great benefit to the other party, because of extraordinary and unpredictable events. The effects of the termination are retroactive to the date of service.

118. Article 474 CC. The expressed resolutory clause dissolves the contract immediately; the tacit clause requires a judicial summons.

119. *See* Anelise Becker, As garantias implícitas no direito brasileiro e em perspectiva comparativista, Revista Direito do Consumidor, Editora RT, São Paulo, nº 09, jan./mar. 1994 pp. 69 et seq.

IV. Penalty Clauses

353. The penalty clause (*cláusula penal*) is an accessory clause, by which an economic sanction in the form of money or another moneywise determinable good is imposed on the party that fails to fulfil an obligation.

354. Although its origin is considered very remote, it was actually elaborated by the Romans who adopted the *stipulatio poenae*, the aim of which was very similar to the penalty clause. There are currently debates regarding the need to rediscover the private penalty, mainly in the Italian doctrine.

355. This clause can be imposed in two different manners: on the one hand, it may be stipulated together with the main obligation, as in Article 409 CC/02. On the other hand, the legislator may authorize the stipulation of the penalty clause separately (as a supplement) or in a posterior act, which can refer to the complete non-performance of the obligation, to the non-performance of a certain clause or simply to delay.

356. The penalty clause is intended to guarantee the performance of the main obligation, settling the losses and gains early, and reinforcing the obligational bond.

357. It should be stressed that this clause must be written and stipulated prior to the non-performance.

358. There are three hypotheses in the Brazilian Civil Code: the non-performance of the contract, a delay and the non-performance of a contract clause.

359. When the penalty clause is stipulated to the hypothesis of the total non-performance of the obligation, it becomes an alternative to the creditor's benefit (Article 410 CC/02). When it is stipulated to the hypothesis of delay or to safeguard another determined clause, the creditor shall have the free choice to impose the fulfilment of the determined penalty along with the performance of the main obligation (Article 411 CC/02).

360. The value of the penalty can be modified by the judge according to Article 413 CC/02, but there is a limit imposed by the law: the value of the penalty imposed by the penalty clause cannot exceed the value of the main obligation.

361. The creditor may refuse to charge a penalty either tacitly in writing or in a tacit way.

362. The fundamental effect of the penalty clause in the legal hypothesis is the immediate enforcement without the need of a judge's decision if the debtor does not perform the obligation or constitutes himself in default, as stipulated in Article 408 CC/02.

363. An interesting solution to situations in which there are many debtors in connection to the same contract is previewed in Articles 414 and 415 CC/02. According to which, all debtors shall be subject to the penalty, if one of them fails to fulfil an indivisible obligation. The non-guilty parties have the right to redress against the party that provoked the penalty application (Article 414 CC/02).

364. However, if the obligation is divisible, only the debtor or his or her heir, that breached the contract, shall be subject to the penalty and proportionally to his or her share of the obligation.

365. To demand the conventional penalty, the creditor is not obliged to claim for losses. Even when the loss exceeds the value of the penalty clause, the creditor cannot claim for a supplementary indemnity if it was not stipulated. If it was stipulated, the value of the penalty clause corresponds to the minimum of the compensation while the creditor has to demonstrate the exceeded losses (Article 416 CC/02[120]).

366. It is important to remark that the penalty clause differs from the right to retraction, because it represents a compensation for the non-fulfilment of a promise.

367. Moreover, it is different from *astreintes,* since these are an injunctive relief imposed by the judge, ex officiis, or by the creditor's claim[121] against a debtor of an obligation which is generally fulfilled day by day. The *astreintes* partially anticipate the restitution of the damages, before they have been proven.

V. Arbitration Clauses

368. Contracts are undoubtedly the most important source of commercial exchange, but, at the same time, they are very often a cause of litigation between the parties. Arbitration is applicable when the parties agree to submit their eventual disputes to an arbitral tribunal, rather than to a State judge. The parties must be capable of contracting and the matter of their dispute must concern the disposal assets.

369. Arbitration law grants the parties the right to choose between the law of the State or Equity[122] to rule their arbitral judgment. This demonstrates the freedom with which the parties can handle their dispute.

120. This article is addressed to the debtor to compel him or her to perform the agreement. The prior settlement of losses is not an issue here, but in its sole §. For further comments on this matter, *see* Antonio Pinto Monteiro, Cláusula penal e Indenização, Coleção Teses, Almedina, Coimbra, 1990, pp. 686 et seq. V. and Judith Martins-Costa, Comentários cit., vol. V, Tomo II, pp. 724 et seq.
121. Foreseen in the New Procedural Code, law n° 13.105 from 16 Mar. 2015, in force on 27 Mar. 2016, Art. 537.
122. There are many theses and a profusion of articles on this subject, among which we would like to refer to a particularly interesting one: *L'Équité* or *les Équités*, confrontation *Occident et Monde Arabe, Société de Législation Comparée*, Paris, 2004.

370. When dissent occurs, the businesses involved often need to quickly find a solution. Arbitration is an excellent tool to prevent and stop litigation, re-establish peace, and allow work to continue, because in the business world, *time is money*. In this regard, the arbitration expert Hans Smit[123] has suggested that we are experiencing a true silent (because most arbitral decisions are not published) revolution in arbitration. The same author considers this behaviour to be typical of a special sector of society, the *Business World.* Nevertheless, the number of litigations submitted to an arbitral tribunal is known to be increasing each year.

371. Concerning Brazilian law, for many years, legislators and national scholars ignored the possibility of resorting to arbitration, due to the misinterpretation of the Federal Constitution, which states that the law shall not exclude any injury or threat to a right from the judicial appreciation.[124] This was interpreted to mean that the courts represented the only means of settling litigation or a dispute.

372. Brazil's first arbitration Law n° 9.307, which was published in 1996, was considered very up to date at that time. Almost twenty years later, Brazil published a new Arbitration Law, Law n° 13.129 on 26 May 2015, which came into force on 27 July 2015.

373. The old law needed a *cure de jeunesse* because the challenges brought about by national and international commerce demanded new forms of justice.

374. The new law provided important innovations in this field, such as the possibility of public administration having recourse to arbitration.[125] Concerning corporations, the law states that an arbitration clause can be included in the articles of association obliging all partners, even dissidents, partners that did not vote and the absentees. The law imposes a quorum of at least 50% of the vote-holding shareholders to approve the arbitration clause. Moreover, the partners opposed to the adoption of such a clause have the right to leave the company and have their shares refunded. In this case, the arbitration clause will come into effect thirty days after the disassociation of such partners.

375. In the arbitration clause, the parties can set out guidelines for an Arbitration Chamber to rule the arbitral judgment. In Brazil, there are many Arbitration Chambers available to the parties, such as the Arbitration Chamber of Brazil-Canada, the CAMARB (The Chamber of Mediation and Arbitration) or the Arbitration Chamber of the FIESP (Federation of Industries of São Paulo) among many others.

---

123. Professor at Columbia Law Faculty, member of *the Société de Législation Comparée*, at a conference in Paris on 15 Mar. 1993.

124. Federal Constitution, Art. 5 XXXV.

125. Nevertheless, the law does not allow the Public Administration to choose between equity or law to rule on a dispute, the only choice is the law. Another imperative rule concerns the mandatory observance of the publicity principle that is a general rule for the activities of Civil Administration.

376. It is important to note that Brazilian arbitration law is monistic; it can regulate national and international arbitrations. Unfortunately, Brazilian law does not allow the use of arbitration to solve disputes involving consumer or employment law. It is interesting to note that in Brazil, arbitration was first forbidden and then criticized mainly by judges for many years. Nowadays, however, it is a very popular and well-known instrument adopted by lawyers and accepted by judges.[126]

§2. Interpretation

377. The interpretation of contracts is one of the most relevant subjects in the General Theory of Contracts, because a contract must be interpreted by the parties, the lawyers and the judges to be executed and to fulfil its goals.

378. For this reason, there is a considerable amount of literature on the subject. According to Emilio Betti, different legal systems have distinct methods of interpreting a contract.[127] In Brazil, the rule originates from Germany, i.e., the interpreter seeks the real content of the will the parties declare. According to Article 112 CC/02, the will of the parties is understood objectively and is to be given more weight than the literal sense.

379. The Italian scholar Natalino Irti explains that the interpretation needs to overcome the literal sense of the language when the parties do not share the same linguistic code. One must go beyond the literal sense because the contract contains a unique code. In order to understand that, the interpreter needs to evaluate the context of the situation as a whole.[128]

380. Moreover, the contract is first interpreted by the parties. However, if they do not agree on the contract's content, the judge will necessarily decide on the correct interpretation.

381. Through the interpretation and with the use of tools like the principle of good faith, uses and customs, the social function of the contract (in Brazilian law), the analogy and the general principles of law, the gaps in the contract are filled and the intentions of the parties become apparent.

126. There are numerous publications referring to this matter; we will mention only the most outstanding: Arnoldo Wald (org.) Doutrinas Essenciais: Arbitragem e Mediação, 07 volumes, Editora Revista dos Tribunais, São Paulo, 2014; Selma Lemes, Arbitragem na Administração Pública, Editora Quartier Latin, São Paulo, 2007; Giovanni Ettore Nanni, Direito Civil e Arbitragem, Editora Atlas, São Paulo, 2014; Leonardo de Faria Beraldo, Curso de Arbitragem, Editora Atlas, São Paulo, 2014; Luiz Fernando do Vale de Almeida Guilherme, Manual de Arbitragem, Editora Método, São Paulo, 2nd edition, 2007.

127. Interpretazione Della Legge e Degli Atti Giuridici, Giuffrè Editore, Milan, 1949.

128. Apud Nelson Rosenvald, Da Interpretação do Negócio Jurídico, in Teoria Geral do Direito Civil, orgs. Renan Lotufo, Giovanni Ettore Nanni, editora Atlas, São Paulo, 2008, pp. 409 et seq.

382. The contract's interpretation rule is governed by Article 113 CC/02 which states that legal affairs must be interpreted pursuant to good faith and the traditions of their place of formation.[129]

383. The person interpreting the contract has to observe the principle of good faith (loyalty between the parties) and *the conservation of the contract,* i.e., if a contract clause is redacted in a way that suggests more than one interpretation, the interpreter will prefer the one that seems to be more useful to the purpose of the agreement.

384. The legislator of the Civil Code elaborated rules[130] to help the parties, lawyers and judges in this difficult task: First, the interpretation of ambiguous or contradictive clauses in adhesion contracts shall be most favourable to the adherent (Article 423 CC/02). Second, the settlement shall be interpreted restrictively (Article 843 CC/02). And third, suretyship contracts do not allow an extensive interpretation (Article 819 CC/02).

§3. Conditional Contracts

385. The field of the Law of Contracts is characterized by private autonomy. The parties can freely determine the form, the content and the terms of their agreements, provided that three limits are observed: public order, the good customs and the social function of the contract (the latter only in Brazilian law).

386. Taking these circumstances into account, the parties can elaborate either aleatory (*contratos aleatórios*) or conditional contracts (*contratos condicionais*), which are similar in some aspects, because, in both contracts, the objective of the agreement may not be achieved. Therefore, it is interesting to establish the differences between these two kinds of agreements.

387. First, it is useful to remember that in commutative contracts, the parties' obligations are certain from the moment of the formation of the contract.

388. In aleatory contracts, the content of the obligation is undetermined, because in this kind of contract, the risk is present in the agreement and the parties agreed with the terms of the contract, without any certainty of gain or loss. For this reason, the obligations could be disproportional, but since the parties are aware of this fact, the agreement is lawful.

389. Now, we can describe the distinction between aleatory and conditional contracts. In a conditional contract, the performance of the contract depends on the

129. *Súmula* n° 409 of the V Journey of the National Council of Justice, CNJ, in 2011 inserted another tool to facilitate the interpretation of contracts: the practices adopted by the parties.
130. These rules concern the interpretation of contracts. In the Civil Code, there are other interpretation rules addressing other kinds of legal relationships.

occurrence of a future event. In contrast to aleatory contracts, in which one of the parties may have profits and the other only losses, in conditional contracts both parties can profit.

390. Moreover, in conditional contracts, the event will always be in the future, while in aleatory contracts, the event can be in the past as long as the result is unknown to the parties; thus, the risk can be said to refer to the future.

391. Summing-up, we can say that a condition is an accidental element of the contract. Normally, contracts are elaborated without conditions. It is defined as the clause, founded exclusively on the parties' wills, which subordinates the efficiency or the resolution of the contract to a future event.[131]

392. The effect of attaching a condition to a contract depends on the kind of condition: if the condition is contingent (*condição suspensiva*), the efficiency of the contract will be interrupted until the event foreseen in the agreement occurs, as stated in Article 125 CC/02. If the condition is resolutory (*condição resolutiva*) the agreement will be extinct when the event foreseen in the contract occurs.

393. Various kinds of conditions can be attached to contracts. Generally, all conditions that do not contradict the law, the public order or the good faith are licit. Among the forbidden conditions are those that deprive the legal transaction of its effects or subject them to the discretion of only one party (Article 122 CC/02).

131. Eduardo Espinola, Manual do Código Civil brasileiro: dos factos jurídicos, dirigido por Paulo de Lacerda, Rio de Janeiro, Ed. J. Ribeiro Santos, 1926, vol. 3, part 2, p. 48, apud Carlos Alberto Dabus Maluf, As Condições no Direito Civil, Editora Saraiva, 3rd edition, 2011, p. 19. Outstanding authors follow the French doctrine in this field: Mathias Latina, Essai sur la condition, LGDJ, Paris, 2009; David Bonnet, Cause et Condition dans les Actes Juridiques, LGDJ, Paris, 2005.

Chapter 4. Privity of Contract

§1. Rule of Privity of Contract

394. According to the Principle of Freedom of Contract and hence Article 421 CC/02, the contracting parties can establish the rules which will govern their contract. Aside from typical contracts, parties may create other contracts (Article 425 CC/02).

395. The effect of the proposal by which a party expresses its willingness to contract is binding when accepted by the other party. The privity of a contract excludes those who do not undertake any obligations, because they are third parties to the contract (*Res inter alios acto, nequet procter, nequet nocet*: a contract is between those who consented).

I. Third Parties and the Contract

396. Under the designation 'Social Function of the Contract' (*função social do contrato*), Article 421 of the Civil Code limits freedom of contract. The notion of functionalization of legal institutions in Brazil is also manifested in ownership and family power. In order for this institute to be effective, it is necessary to identify the law and its purpose, as well as the consequences in case of infringements.

397. Regarding contracts, it is said that the freedom of contract shall give rise to useful and fair dealings.[132]

398. The Social Function of Contracts configures the following exceptions to the binding and privative effects of the freedom of contract: opposability, which is enforcing the contract against third parties to the contract, as exemplified by Professor Junqueira de Azevedo;[133] and extensibility, which is the most intense form of forcing others to obey the performance of contracts, requiring third parties to comply with contractual obligations, as exemplified by statement (*súmula*) 308 of the Superior Court of Justice (STJ), according to which a creditor bank may not require a buyer's property if he or she has paid the amount due to the property developer.

132. Jacques Ghestin, L'Utile et le Juste dans les Contrats, Archives de Philosophie du Droit, 26: 35 (1982).

133. Princípios do novo direito contratual e desregulamentação do mercado, Revista dos Tribunais, n. 750, April 1998, São Paulo, p. 116.

II. Contract for the Benefit of a Third Party (*contratos em favor de terceiros*)

399. Stipulation in favour of a third party is an institution contained in Roman law. Third parties benefit from advantages arising from the contract which is governed by Articles 436–438 CC/02. Examples are life insurance and health insurance policies.

§2. Transfer of Contractual Rights

400. It is possible to assign the rights and obligations of a contract to another person (*cessão do contrato*). However, depending on the content of the clause, this may only be possible with authorization or entirely forbidden. Transferable obligations may be transferred; personal obligations may not.

§3. Special Case: Subcontracts

401. Subcontracting (*subcontratação*) differs from the cession of contract rights, in which the title of a party is replaced. When subcontracting, a part of the obligation is transferred to a third party.

§4. *Actio Pauliana*

402. Fraud is characterized by two requirements: *Consilium fraudis*: bad faith (i.e., the knowledge of fraud) present in the act of fraud against creditors; and *Eventus damni*: prejudice to a pre-existing creditor.

403. Nowadays, some authors argue that it is unnecessary to prove *consilium fraudis* in more serious cases, such as the fraudulent donation (which is more serious than the fraudulent sale of assets, which may be made to obtain money to pay off debts). In the case of fraud in fraudulent onerous transactions, it still has to be proven that the insolvency was notorious or that the other party (which acquired the assets) was aware of it.

404. There are several cases of fraud against creditors provided for in the Civil Code which do not exclude the existence of specific legislation. Those expressed in the Civil Code are transactions for the free transfer of assets or forgiveness of debt (Article 158 CC/02), fraudulent onerous transactions (Article 159 CC/02), fraudulent anticipation of payment (Article 162 CC/02), fraudulent granting of a security guarantee (Article 163 CC/02) and fraudulent institution of assets as protected family assets (Article 1.711 CC/02). Transactions involving the free transfer of assets or the forgiveness of debt may be nullified by unsecured creditors or creditors whose guarantees are found to be insufficient to cover the debts, if the transactions are practised by insolvent debtor or if they cause insolvency, even when in ignorance. Only those who were creditors at the time of such acts may request their annulment (Article 158 CC/02).

405. Onerous contracts of an insolvent debtor shall also be voidable if the insolvency is evident or if there is reason for the other contracting party to be aware of it (Article 159 CC/02).

406. The unsecured creditor who receives payment of a debt that has not yet expired from an insolvent debtor shall return it to be shared among the creditors (Article 162 CC/02).

407. The rights of the other creditors regarding debt guarantees that the insolvent debtor may have given to any creditor are presumed to be fraudulent (Article 163 CC/02).

408. The invalidity of fraudulent transactions is sought via *actio pauliana*, which is personal (not in rem) and has a statute of limitations of four years.

409. After the annulment of fraudulent transactions, the resulting advantage shall be reversed to the benefit of the acquis for it to be shared among the creditors. If the only object of such transactions was the assignment of preferential rights, through mortgage, pledge or other guarantees, its invalidity shall only void such preferential rights (Article 165 CC/02).

Chapter 5. Termination of Contract

§1. Performance and Breach

410. Default or breach of contract can be caused by an express provision, in which case the termination of the contract occurs by law (*ope legis*).

411. Doctrine and case law both allow the invocation of substantive due performance. It may occur tacitly, in which case the contract terminates *ope iudicis*, that is, by court decision, which must be absolute.

§2. Impossibility, Frustration and Hardship: The Unforeseen

412. 'Resolution' (*resolução*) is the technical term for the termination of a contract due to failure of the debtor. The rule is not absolute: certain defaults cannot result in a termination, because the debtor is entitled to pay, including via judicial deposit (so that the debtor who wants to pay can force the creditor to receive).

413. Some defaults may be overcome. However, there are three types of termination: expressed termination, implied termination, and termination due to economic causes.

414. An expressed termination is written into contractual clauses. The basic rule is that the parties can override a relative default (not expressly provided).

415. Implied termination occurs when both the debtor and the creditor are in default because the debtor does not make the payment and the creditor refuses to receive it either at the time and/or place and/or in the manner prescribed by law or established convention (Article 394 CC/02).

416. Termination due to economic causes is foreseen in Article 478 CC/02, which states that in contracts of continuous or deferred performance, the debtor may request the termination of the contract, if the debt of one party becomes excessively onerous with great benefit to the other party, because of extraordinary and unpredictable events. The effects of the termination are retroactive to the date of service.

§3. Discharge by Agreement

417. Denúncia is the termination of a contract by agreement. It is made in the same manner required by the contract (Article 472 CC/02). The use of the same manner used in the original contract is the only requirement for valid termination by reverting to the *status quo ante*.

Chapter 6. Remedies

§1. General Provisions

418. Generally, people perform their contractual obligations for many reasons. The most important reason is grounded on an ancient rule of Roman origin and later revived by Canonical law, expressed in the sentence *pacta sunt servanda* (agreements must be kept).

419. Citizens conceive the contract as a tool to plan and organize their economic life during a certain period of time. That is why the French doctrine considers *the contract as an act of forecast.* This point of view is in accordance with a conception of contract related to the protection of the parties by which the legal system needs to assure security to the parties.

420. Another important aspect of this conception of contract is a *brocard* which states that a contract is a law between the parties. That is to say, the matter of the contract is imposed on the parties in the same way that the law is imposed on all citizens, obliging them to obey.

421. Looking at the various characteristics of contracts, especially their obligatory force (no one enters into a contract against his or her own will) we will notice that the parties must perform the contract, which is an agreement that is normally unchangeable by one party, because it has an obligatory force. Nevertheless, if both parties decide to modify or to revoke their agreement, they may do so.

422. All these requirements regarding contracts have their origin in Article 422 of the Civil Code of 2002, which states that when signing the contract as well as during the performance of the contract, both parties must adhere to the principles of probity and good faith.

423. When, unfortunately, for any reason, one party does not fulfil the terms of a contract, the affected party can use the legal remedies and mitigate any losses accrued.

§2. Specific Performance and Injunctions: *Astreintes*

424. The Brazilian law does not foresee the concept of specific performance. It was introduced first by scholars and then by the courts.

425. Clóvis do Couto e Silva[134] introduced this common law concept to Brazilian lawyers and judges, in an article, in which he commented the concept of *substantial performance*, explaining that it means a performance of the contract very close to the final result originally foreseen by both parties when signing the contract.

426. Consequently, depending on the parties' behaviour, the right of resolution must be excluded. Nevertheless, the aggrieved party has the right to claim an indemnity.[135] This solution is based on the principle of good faith.

427. As pointed out by Araken de Assis, this concept has a different sense and a smaller sphere of application in Brazil since it was imported. Indeed, in Brazilian doctrine and courts, the conception of substantial performance is equivalent to a kind of non-performance, which is called *bad performance* (*mau cumprimento/mau inadimplemento contratual*). It is the task of the judge to estimate if the partial performance is beneficial to the creditor, as stated in Article 395 CC/02.[136]

428. To evaluate if the performance was substantial, the judge analyses the consequences produced by the non-performance of the contract and the relevance of the unperformed clause for both parties.

429. The leading case concerning this matter was decided by Justice Ruy Rosado de Aguiar Jr., at the Rio Grande do Sul State Court, in which the creditor in a works contract which was poorly performed sought resolution of the contract, grounded on the concept of non-performance. The tribunal decided to maintain the contract, granting the creditor the right to recover his losses by the payment of an indemnity by the debtor (the builder).[137]

430. The Superior Tribunal of Justice (*STJ*), the court whose responsibility is to assure the harmonization of jurisprudence throughout the country, recognizes the reception and application of the substantial performance principle in Brazil,[138] as a consequence of the general interpretation of the principle of good faith and the social function of the contract.

---

134. O Princípio da Boa Fé no Direito Brasileiro e Português, Estudos de Direito Civil brasileiro e português, org. por Marcello Caetano, José Carlos Moreira ALVES, Clóvis do Couto e SILVA e Mário Júlio de Almeida Costa, ed. Revista dos Tribunais, São Paulo, 1980, pp. 42 et seq. esp. p. 56.
135. This situation was regulated in the former Civil Code by Art. 1.092 and its sole §: If the contract is not performed completely, the creditor can choose between imposing the performance or resolving the contract.
136. Resolução do Contrato por Inadimplemento, editor Revista dos Tribunais, São Paulo, 4th edition, 2004, p. 134.
137. 5a. Câmara Cível TJRGS, 2 May 1989, Ap.Civ.n. 589016534.
138. Superior Tribunal de Justiça. REsp 877.965. Relator: Ministro Luis Felipe Salomão, Quarta Turma, judged on 22 Nov. 2011. Online: http://www.stj.jus.br/webstj/processo/justica/detalhe.asp?numreg =200601803559. Superior Tribunal de Justiça. REsp 953.389. Relatora: Ministra Nancy Andrighi, Terceira Turma, judged on 23 Feb. 2010. Online http://www.stj.jus.br/webstj/processo/Justica/ detalhe.asp?numreg=200701157039&pv=00000000000. -Superior Tribunal de Justiça. REsp 1.05 1.270. Relator: Ministro Luis Felipe Salomão, Quarta Turma, judged on 04/08/2011. Online http:

431. Brazilian procedural law allows for *astreintes*, which are intended to ensure that there is a certain behaviour or omission on the part of the bound party, by applying a kind of psychological pressure imposed, to fulfil the promised obligation.

432. It is unanimously understood that the value of the *astreintes* may be higher than the value of a penalty clause that may exist in the contract.

433. The imposition of the *astreintes* by the judge must show that it is better for the bound party to perform the judge's decision. As stated in Article 551 of the recently published Brazilian Procedural Civil Code, the periodic penalty payment does not depend on the party's requirement and can be granted in the discovery phase, in an injunction or advance protection or decision or moreover, during the enforcement proceedings, as long as it is enough and consistent with the obligation in the judge's opinion. A reasonable extension will be determined to allow the fine to be paid. The §1 of Article 551 says that the judge can, ex officio or on the party's request, modify the value and the periodicity of the fine or exclude it, without retroactive effect, if it is found to be insufficient or excessive, or if the bound party performed the obligation partially or if there is a fair cause for non-performance. Article 551 also states that the value of the fine belongs to the prevailing party. The definitive payment of the fine depends on the judge's final decision. The fine is due from the day on which the non-payment was detected and will be imposed until the obligation is met. Nevertheless, a provisional fulfilment of the decision that states the fine is allowed, when applicable.

§3. Termination

434. The termination of a contract is very similar to the end of a human being's life, because just like a life, a contract has a beginning, a certain duration in time and one day, it will end by different forms of extinction.

435. It has been pointed out by Professor Álvaro Villaça de Azevedo,[139] a contract may be terminated first, due to a previously existent imperfection, which results in the nullity or the voidance of the contract. An example is a contract signed by a 15-year-old or a contract with an illicit aim. Second, a contract may be terminated due to the fulfilment of all its obligations, normally by payment. Third, negligent non-performance can lead to the unilateral or bilateral termination of the contract. Bilateral termination of the contract is a discharge by agreement (*distrato*). Lastly, involuntary non-negligent non-performance may lead to the resolution of a contract, when, for example, the object of the contract disappears. A

//www.stj.jus.br/webstj/processo/justica/detalhe.asp?numreg=200800893455. -Superior Tribunal de Justiça. REsp 1.200.105. Relator: Ministro Paulo de Tarso Sanseverino, Terceira Turma, judged on 19 Jun. 2012. Online: http://www.stj.jus.br/webstj/processo/justica/detalhe.asp?numreg=201001113350.

139. Princípios Contratuais no Novo Código Civil, Débora Gozzo, José Carlos Moreira Alves, Miguel Reale (org.), Editora Saraiva, 2006, p. 10.

contract is over when, for instance, a fire destroys the object of a sales contract or if the debtor whose obligation has a strictly personal nature dies before performing it.

436. There is another situation of contract rupture, previewed by the Brazilian Civil Code (Articles 478 and 480) grounded on the effective disproportion between the parties' obligations (*eccessiva onerosità*). As mentioned above, Article 478 states that in contracts of continuous or deferred performance, the debtor may request the termination of the contract, if the debt of one party becomes excessively onerous with great benefit to the other party, because of extraordinary and unpredictable events. The effects of the termination are retroactive to the date of service.

437. It is important to remark that this kind of resolution is admitted only in the hypothesis of a commutative contract of continuous or deferred execution and in the case of the occurrence of extraordinary and unforeseeable events.

438. Despite the importance of this doctrine and the large number of cases identified in the comparative law research (with emphasis on the Italian and German courts), the Brazilian Civil Code has been very parsimonious and excessively cautious when authorizing its application.

439. As we can easily deduce from Article 480 CC/02, the Brazilian Civil Code adopted the Italian doctrine of the *eccessiva onerosità,* the excessive burden: if, according to the contract, only one of the parties has to perform obligations, he or she could plead to reduce the obligation or to change the manner of performing it, in order to prevent an excessive burden.

440. The Brazilian legislator allows the possibility of revising a contract. Article 317 CC/02 provides that when, due to unforeseeable reasons a clear disproportion between the value of the debt and the time of its performance arises, the judge may correct it upon request of the party in order to secure, as far as possible, the real value of the debt.

441. The drafting of Article 479 CC/02, which says that the resolution of the contract can be avoided if the defendant proposes to change the contract conditions in a fair manner, shows that the legislator intended to preserve the contract.

442. Still, the rule is to terminate the deal in case of a non-performance of the contract.

443. Incidentally, some legal experts[140] have a different understanding of this matter, saying that the legislator could adopt a broad concept of the *eccessiva onerosità,* for example, authorizing the judge to apply it ex officio, and not only on a party's request, as is stated in the Civil Code. Moreover, that author suggests that this theory could also be applied to any contract in which there is undue imbalance.

140. Op. mentioned, p. 15.

§4. *Exceptio Non Adimpleti Contracts*

444. Bilateral or synallagmatic contracts, whose obligations are related, admit certain mechanisms that other kinds of contracts, like unilateral contracts in which only one party has a burden, do not allow. Only bilateral contracts admit the *exceptio non adimpleti contractus* and the *tacit resolutory clause*.[141]

445. In bilateral contracts, none of the parties can demand the performance of the other party before the performance of its own obligation. This rule is grounded on the principle of synallagma, e.g., the mutual dependence between the obligations in a contract. Nevertheless, there is a norm that regulates the right to invoke the *exceptio non adimpleti contractus*: it can only be invoked when neither the law nor the contract determines who must perform first.

446. If the performance is successive, the party that must perform first can only refuse to do so if there is a reason to suppose that the other party will not perform.

447. Such behaviour will be admitted if the party that must perform first knows that the other will not perform, because it is unable to do so or suffers from economic problems such as financial loss. In such circumstances, the party that would be the first to perform can refuse to do so until the other provides a reliable guarantee of its ability to fulfil its contractual obligations.

448. There is another remedy that can be invoked in the case of an incomplete or defective performance: *exceptio non rite adimpleti contractus,*[142] for instance, when one of the parties has partially performed the obligation or when an already completely performed obligation was defective. At first glance, both obligations seem to be similar, but their consequences differ: in the hypothesis of total non-performance, the proof of this faulty behaviour must be presented by the party that did not perform its obligation. In the hypothesis of partial non-performance, the proof must be presented by the party that invokes the *exceptio*.

449. Concerning the nature of the *exceptio,* the Romans used to say that it is an authentic right, but scholars like Ennecerus[143] argue that it is a counter-right. The

141. Article 476 CC. In bilateral contracts, neither party is allowed to ask for the fulfilment of the obligation by the other party before fulfilling its own obligation.

Article 477 CC. If after the conclusion of the contract, one of the contracting parties suffers a decrease in his or her patrimony that may jeopardize or put into question the promised instalment, the other party can refuse to perform his or her instalment, until the other party fulfils the one he or she is responsible for or gives a sufficient guarantee of its ability to fulfill it.

142. This denomination was given by in the German Civil Code, paras 320 and 321, according to SALAS, Acdeel, De la exception non adimpleti contractus, Revista de Jurisprudencia Argentina, 62/679, apud Hugo Taranto, in Contratos, book organized by Felix Trigo Represas y Ruben Stiglitz, Ediciones La Rocca, Buenos Aires, 1989, p. 260, note 03.

143. Ennecerus, Kipp e Wolff, Tratado de Derecho Civil, t. II, p. 166, apud Orlando Gomes, Contratos, Editora Forense, Rio de Janeiro, 1991, 12th edition, p. 100. *See also* Álvaro Villaça de Azevedo, Teoria Geral dos Contratos Típicos e Atípicos, editora Atlas, São Paulo, 3rd edition, p. 88.

juridical base for the *exceptio* differs in the doctrine: it may be the cause theory,[144] the equity, the prohibition of illicit enrichment or the theory of the necessary balance between both obligations.

450. A different scenario is possible: the party that did not perform imposes the performance on the other party. The juridical solution for the party that suffered the loss is to terminate the contract and to claim damages pursuant to statutory requirements.

451. It is important to stress that this solution is only possible when the performance of the obligation becomes impossible. If this is not the case and the nature of the obligation admits such a solution, the party can claim a coercive enforcement procedure.

452. Based on the principle of private autonomy, the parties are allowed to abdicate the *exceptio* when signing the contract.

453. Lastly, the *exceptio* cannot be invoked, when the contract contains the clause *solve et repetere (pay and complain later).* Nowadays, the *exceptio non adimpleti contractus* is a very important legal institute, because it is in accordance with the principle of solidarity upon which the Brazilian Civil Code is built.[145]

§5. Faulty Behaviour of the Debtor

454. If we compare the current Brazilian Civil Code to the former one, in which the legislator did not include any chapter on rupture or the termination of contract, we will observe that the legislator of the current Code of 2002 provided new rules concerning this matter and changed the way it was understood.[146]

455. The debtor's non-performance is defined by Professor Menezes Cordeiro[147] as the non-performance of the duties to perform in favour of the creditor, at the time, place and form established by the law or by the agreement.

---

144. In France, this remedy (suspension of the creditor's performance) is grounded on the theory of cause, because in a synallagmatic contract, each obligation is the cause of the other. *See* prof. Joana Schmidt, IEL, FRANCE, Kluwer International, 1999, pp. 182 and 183.
145. Max Scheler's Phenomenology of Solidarism 'The Third Path' of Normative Political Philosophy Wei Zhang Sun Yat-sen University.
146. The doctrine stresses that the new Code, in this special field, constitutes a remarkable improvement, because it adopts a system that allows a better view of Miguel Reale's conception of non-performance. In Art. 389, we can visualize the general and typical effect of the non-performance of an obligation or a contract, that is to say, the debtor is liable and must pay losses and damages etc. *See* more on this matter in Judith Martins-Costa, (org. Sálvio de Figueiredo Teixeira), Comentários ao Novo Código Civil, do Inadimplemento das Obrigações, Arts 389–420, vol. V, tomo II, 2nd edition, Editora Forense, Rio de Janeiro, 2009, pp. 126 et seq.
147. Direito das Obrigações, Lisboa: Associação Acadêmica da Faculdade de Direito de Lisboa, 1980, p. 436.

456. Faulty behaviour on the part of the debtor acquired a stronger meaning with the adoption of the lateral duties doctrine originating in the German tradition (*Nebenpflichten*). Main duties and accessories or ancillary duties are enforceable, and the debtor can also be liable for their non-performance. It is important to note that technically the word *duty* refers to a legal obligation, something that the party or both parties have to accomplish regardless of their will, while *obligation* is an agreement settled by two or more parties, whose content is composed of different obligations chosen by them.

457. The new Brazilian Civil Code recognizes the non-performance of secondary duties as faulty behaviour on the part of the debtor, because the principle of good faith is considered to apply to all obligations under the contract.

458. The Civil Code provides general provisions about this matter, as seen in Article 389 CC/02. The debtor is liable for the consequences of his or her faulty behaviour, such as losses and damages plus interest according to regularly established official monetary adjustment indexes, and legal fees if he or she does not perform his or her obligation.

459. The non-performance of the debtor's duties and obligations causes termination of the contract as stated in Article 474 CC/02, as mentioned above.

460. When, however, breach of contract has been characterized, the debtor has the burden to demonstrate that he or she is not responsible for the damage.[148]

461. There are two kinds of non-performance by faulty behaviour: absolute non-performance (when the performance of the obligation became impossible) and relative non-performance (when the debtor can somehow perform the obligation).

462. In Brazilian law, there are also two kinds of relative non-performance: default and positive breach of an obligation.[149] Delay in performing a contract obligation is called default (*mora*).[150] The debtor is considered to be in default, when he or she does not pay his or her debt, while a creditor is in default, when he or she refuses to receive the payment at the time, the place and manner prescribed by law or convention (Article 394 CC/02).

463. The conditions for a positive breach (*violação positiva*) of obligation or contract are an apparent impression that: (1) the terms of the contract have not been fulfilled; (2) the terms of the contract have been defectively fulfilled; (3) there is no regulation regarding the defective fulfilment; and (4) there are material damages unrelated to delay and/or impossibility.

148. *Súmula* no. 06, Civil Law Journey, Brasília, DF., September 2013.
149. *See* Renata C. Steiner, Descumprimento Contratual, boa fé e violação positiva do contrato, Quartier Latin, São Paulo, 2014.
150. There is a difference of meaning between *delay* and *slowing* [*retardamento*]: delay [*mora*] is a faulty slowing, while regular slowing is not faulty and can produce juridical effects like lapse and prescription.

464. These four conditions constitute a positive breach of contract or obligation resulting in the termination of the contract and the possibility of claiming damages.

465. Nowadays, the Brazilian courts consider the non-performance of an accessory duty or obligation, the anticipatory refusal to perform the contract, the non-performance of negative obligations and the non-performance of singular obligations as a violation of the creditor's rights and therefore a positive breach of contract.

466. According to this point of view, the Brazilian Superior Tribunal of Justice, STJ, elaborated the following Súmula:[151] due to the principle of Good Faith, foreseen in Article 422 CC/02, the violation of the secondary duties constitutes non-performance, regardless of fault.

467. According to Brazilian doctrine, Article 394 CC/02 provides for a broader concept of penalty, because the positive breach of contract is also included in this concept of faulty delay.[152]

468. The regulation of losses and damages to be paid by the debtor constitutes a relevant matter that the legislator tried to regulate as precisely as possible, as we can *see* in Articles 402, 403, 404 and 405 CC/02.

469. Article 402 states that besides the exceptions in the law, the damages and losses due to the creditor shall cover what was actually lost and the profit the creditor reasonably failed to make.

470. According to Article 403, the losses and damages shall include only the damages and the effective loss of profit arising directly from the non-performance, without prejudice to the content of the procedural law, even if the non-performance is a consequence of the debtor's fraud.

471. Under Article 404 CC/02, losses and damages in obligations that are paid in cash shall be paid according to the official monetary adjustment index, encompassing interest and legal fees. Default interest is counted from the original summons (Article 405 CC/02).

472. In order to give a broad insight into the regulation of this matter in the Civil Code, it is important to refer to two other articles: Article 406 CC/02 governs that if the parties did not agree on any default interest or if no interest rate was stipulated or if there are legal interest rates, they shall be fixed pursuant to the existing rates for default tax payment to the National Treasury.

151. *Súmula* n. 24, First Civil Law Workshop, Brasília, DF, September, 2002.
152. *See* Gustavo Kratz Gazalle, O conceito de mora no Código Civil de 2002, Sérgio Antonio Fabris editor, Porto Alegre, 2008.

473. Article 407 CC/02 says that even without any allegation of loss, the debtor is obliged to pay default interest calculated in cash in the case of monetary debts and in kind for other debts, if the value was not determined by a court decision, arbitration or agreement between the parties.

§6. Limitation of Actions

474. This matter is regulated differently in different legal systems and traditions. In Brazilian law, the Civil Code regulates the limitation action, while in the UK, for example, there is the Limitation Act of 1983. Nevertheless, some rules have the same or at least similar origins, despite belonging to two different legal traditions, such as the Roman-German or Civil Law Family or the Common Law.

475. Regarding limitation actions, Brazil and the UK share the same definition: the Limitation Act of the UK and the Brazilian Civil Code set out the rules on how long a creditor has to take a certain action against the debtor to recover a debt. In both systems, time limits do not apply to all types of recovery action. Moreover, the time limitations are different depending on the type of debt.

476. Limitation periods for debts are important, because if the creditor has run out of time, it is possible that the debt will not be paid.[153]

477. The limitation can be set as the effect of the time that covers the entitlement, without extinguishing the right or the contract. Indeed, a debt that passed its statute of limitations cannot be requested by the creditor, because after some time, due to his negligent behaviour, the creditor loses the right to charge the debtor (the Romans used to say *dormientibus non sucurrit jus*). Nevertheless, in the field of ethics, the debt still remains unpaid. In such circumstances, Brazilian law[154] considers it lawful if the debtor pays his or her debt spontaneously. The debtor has no right to recover this money, nor is the creditor obliged to give back the amount.

478. The main rule in the Brazilian Civil Code of 2002 regarding the limitation of actions is in Article 205, which states that the period is ten years unless the law provides a shorter period.

479. Article 206 of the Civil Code regulates specific limitation periods of one, two or more years. The duration depends on the kind of right.

480. In law, another time-related factor is lapse (*decadência*), which is defined as the cause of the extinction of a right (not a claim) because it was not exercised in the period stipulated by the law.

---

153. Rodrigo Xavier Leonardo, 'A prescrição no Código Civil Brasileiro (ou o jogo dos sete erros)', Revista da Faculdade de Direito da Universidade Federal do Paraná, v. 51, pp. 101–120, 2010.
154. Article 882 CC. An amount that has been paid to cancel a debt that passed its statute of limitation or to fulfil an obligation that is legally unenforceable cannot be taken back.

481. Unless otherwise specified by law, the prescription rules concerning its prevention, suspension and interruption do not apply to lapse (Article 207 CC/02).

482. The new Civil Code tried to shorten all the limitation periods of the former code. The reasons for this change are diverse, while the main factor, however, was the way that life had changed: scientific progress facilitated communication and modern means of transport reduced the time needed to travel long distances. Thus, nowadays, no one can allege to not have found his or her debtor to collect a debt.

483. The limitation period begins to count from the date on which the claimant's cause of action accrued.

484. It is important to note that this matter touches two kinds of law: material and procedural law. There are some rights that never prescribe, i.e., when the entitlement derives from a constitutive action exercised without delay. According to the law, these rights are perpetual; they can be judged at any time by a court of law, an example being the claim for divorce.[155]

§7. Damages and Exemption Clauses

485. Damages and exemption clauses are the subjects of ongoing debate, because they offend the spirit of the obligations and contracts due to the fact they are signed to be performed and if they are not, the guilty party is liable.

486. More conservative authors consider the insertion of such clauses in the contract a violation of the public order.

487. Nevertheless, such exemption clauses are not uncommon, for instance in parking areas, where a sign states that the provider is not responsible for any damage that may be suffered by cars in the parking lot. This declaration is not efficient, because the enterprise that offers this service to the consumer has the obligation to take care of the cars parked in the building, because such a service must be safe to be offered on the market.[156]

488. Generally, the non-performance of an obligation triggers a liability for the damages. There is, however, another way to look at this problem which originates with liberalism – a doctrine that grants great freedom to the society and aims at the exclusion of the State from private relationships. According to this thought, there is

155. For further information on this matter in Brazilian law, *see* Humberto Theodoro Junior, 'Da prescrição e decadência no novo Código Civil brasileiro', in Aspectos Controvertidos do novo Código Civil, estudos em homenagem ao Ministro José Carlos Moreira Alves, Editora Revista dos Tribunais, São Paulo, 2003, pp. 315 et seq.

156. The Brazilian Consumer Protection Code in Art. 8 states that the products and services put on the consumer market shall not create any damages to the health or the safety of the consumer, except these considered normal and predictable due to its nature and fruition; in any case, the supplier is obliged to provide the necessary and suitable information about it.

no problem if two or more capable and free people decide to exclude the State, and exercise their options, for example, eliminating liability in their contract.

489. Brazilian law allows that in a work contract, both parties agree that if the work is not finished at the time they agreed, the contractor will not be responsible, as Article 51, I of the Consumer Protection Code states.

490. But the exemption clauses include some nuances, as we can see in this example of the works contract: the constructor cannot be exempted from ensuring the work is safe.

491. Generally, equal parties can agree on an exemption or the limitation of liability in case of non-performance of contract obligations. If one of the parties is not a consumer, the clause of liability cannot be excluded, and such a clause is considered void.[157]

§8. Restitution

492. Restitution (*restituição*)[158] is a remedy available in many civil lawsuits. It consists in calculating the gains of the defendant and the corresponding losses of the plaintiff. The gains of the defendant must have been lawfully obtained.

493. This remedy is applied when someone has an undue profit on account of another person's loss (*enriquecimento sem causa*). Consequently, the legislator regulates such an unfair situation by a legal procedure intended to restore the original economic status of both parties.

494. In Brazilian law, Article 884 of the Civil Code of 2002 states that a person, who without a fair cause becomes rich at the expense of another person, is obliged to refund what has been unjustly obtained, with the value corrected according to inflation. In the sole paragraph of this article, the legislator established rules on how to refund the undue profit: if the enrichment consists in a determined good, the receiver must return it; and, if the thing no longer exists, the restitution will be made according to the value of the good at the time it was required.

495. To claim unjust enrichment, the claimant must demonstrate the real enrichment of the defendant; the existence of a loss on the part of the claimant; and the existence of a causal link between the loss suffered and the undue profit. Restitution is not only due when there is no cause to justify the enrichment but also when the

157. About this subject, *see* Arnoldo Wald, A Cláusula de limitação de Responsabilidade no direito brasileiro, Revista e Direito Civil Contemporâneo, n. 2, v. 4, pp. 131–138; São Paulo, editora RT, jul./set. 2015.
158. On this subject *see* Cláudio Fortunato MICHELON Junior, Direito Restitutório: enriquecimento sem causa, pagamento indevido, gestão de negócios, Editora RT, São Paulo, 2007.

cause no longer exists (Article 885 CC/02). If the law provides other ways for the aggrieved party to compensate the suffered loss, the restitution due to enrichment is not possible (Article 886 CC/02).

496. The aggrieved person has three years to file the lawsuit against the party that wrongfully profited at his or her expense (Article 206 IV CC/02).

497. Unjust enrichment is, however, not the only situation where restitution is due. We can also refer to the *undue payment* (*pagamento indevido*) and the *business management* (the management of another person's affairs without empowerment, *gestão de negócios*).

498. Undue payment[159]is another possible cause for *actio in rem verso* (restitution); it is regulated in Articles 876–883 of the Civil Code.

499. Article 876 defines 'undue payment' as something that a person receives that was not due to him or her. He or she is obliged to refund it, and this obligation is imposed on the person who receives a conditional debt before the fulfilment of the condition.

500. Moreover, Article 877 adds that a person who involuntarily paid something undue has to demonstrate that he or she did so by mistake.

501. According to Article 879, the legislator takes the good or the bad faith of who received this payment into account. If someone unduly received a real estate and sold it in good faith, onerously, he or she is only liable for the received amount. However, if the person acted in bad faith, he or she shall also be held liable for losses and damages. Someone who unduly received a payment as a part of a true debt, but destroyed the documentary proof or let the debt prescribe or gave up the guarantees of his or her rights, is not obliged to refund the undue payment, but the person who paid it disposes of a regressive action (action *in rem verso*) against the actual debtor and his or her guarantor (Article 880 CC/02).

502. Restitution is also due in case of *business management* or the management of another person's affairs without the empowerment to do so. Article 861 of the Civil Code foresees that someone who intervenes in the management of another person's affairs without his or her empowerment must handle those affairs according to the presumptive interest and will of the owner, being liable for that person and people with whom he or she will treat.

503. The management of another person's affairs without empowerment is similar to the tacit mandate (*mandato*), which, however, includes a previous agreement between the owner and the agent. In the case of undue business management, there

159. *See* Clóvis do Couto e Silva, A Teoria da Causa no Direito Privado, in Vera Jacob de Fradera (org.) O Direito Privado Brasileiro na Visão de Clóvis do Couto e Silva, Editora Livraria do Advogado, Porto Alegre, 2015, 2nd edition, pp. 57 et seq.

is no previous agreement. The contact between parties is hazardous. Sometimes, there is no contact at all, but only the circumstances indicate a relation. This might, for example, be the case during a trip by train, when two persons sitting in the same compartment begin to talk and to exchange information. They give each other personal data and speak about their business activities. Suddenly, one of them suffers a heart attack and dies. The other begins to take actions, to inform the family, workplace and lawyer of the deceased traveller in order to inform them about the facts. If he incurs any expenses for taking all these providences, he will be reimbursed by the deceased's heirs.

504. If the management was initiated against the manifested or presumed will of the interested person, the person who did so will be held liable even for the acts of God, if he or she did not prove that these facts could occur, even if he or she had abstained.

Part II. Specific Contracts

Chapter 1. Agency

§1. Introduction

505. As is widely known, commercial activity concerns the movement of goods in the economic chain (production and consumption), such as purchase and sale agreements: the manufacturer produces goods for the market, which other people – traders – acquire for resale in the market.

506. In the past, the craftsmen sold their goods directly to consumers. Later, manufacturers instructed certain employees to find new customers in other places, giving rise to travelling salespeople who, though linked to the manufacturing company, were physically separated from it.

507. Today, with advances in industrialization, the manufacturer may be unable to reach the whole consumer market and therefore employ people specifically to sell the product. The entrepreneur may also seek people apart from his or her own employees to do this work, such as other business owners, giving rise to the figure of the *commercial representation* or *agency* (business cooperation contracts).

508. The business environment led to the figure of the autonomous agent, who commands and organizes their own company without any interference from manufacturers, who use their services. Thus, the profession of 'agent' developed to intermediate business. Under Brazilian law, those who practised this activity were officially referred to as *autonomous trade representative* (*representante comercial autônomo*, Law n° 4.886/65).

509. The 2002 Civil Code abandoned that name and instead adopted that of 'agent' (*agente*), who, however, exercises exactly the same functions as in the past.

§2. Agency and Distribution Agreements

510. The Civil Code refers to agency and distribution agreements (*contrato de agência e distribuição*), although they are the same thing, the only difference being that with distribution, the functions of the sales agency are broader.

511. The word 'distribution' is very broad and carries numerous meanings. In the strictest sense, such as under Article 710 CC/02, distribution is a service, which differs from the reselling function of the agent. The distributor is a service provider whose economic and legal function is to attract customers. According to doctrine, the distributor is a keeper of the tenderer's goods, who performs all the steps involved in the distribution business on behalf of the company he or she represents. A distributor is not a salesperson, but rather, an agent of the seller.

512. Such an agreement is not to be confused with a 'commercial concession contract' (*contrato de concessão comercial*), which, according to Requião,[160] is an atypical, bilateral and commutative contract of mixed or complex formulation. By contrast, distribution agreements involve an agent.

I. Definition of the Agency and Distribution Agreement

513. When entering an agency or commercial representation agreement, a person – the agent – takes on the obligation to offer certain goods and/or services, within a certain geographical area, on a non-sporadic basis independently, and on behalf of someone else – the tenderer or supplier – in exchange for payment.

514. The definition of Article 710 CC/02 contains elements that specify the activity of an agent, reinforcing the autonomous nature of the contractual figure by excluding other information in order to avoid confusion with the figure of the commercial representative, who is typically an employee.[161]

515. The core of the activity translates into the verb 'promote' (*promover*). The word 'represent' would perhaps be more accurate, but since the law on commercial representation uses this term, the Civil Code adopted an alternative verb.

II. Characteristics of Agency and Distribution Agreements

516. Agency and distribution agreements are relationships between business people. There is no hierarchical dependency between the agent (representor) and the representee, as the agent acts autonomously in the conduct and organization of his or her business. Another distinguishing feature is that the objective of the contract is not for a specific event or contract, but rather, a common practice, establishing a lasting bond between the agent and the representee. Representation includes acts conducted by one party on behalf of another, constituting brokerage. The rendering

160. See Rubens Requião, O contrato de concessão de venda com exclusividade (concessão comercial), Revista da Faculdade de Direito UFPR, 1972, pp. 207–246.

161. *See* Araken de Assis, Contratos Nominados, Ed RT, São Paulo, 2005, p. 197; *see also* Francisco Cavalcanti Pontes de Miranda, 'Tratado de Direito Privado', 1984, 3rd edition, São Paulo, RT, vol. 44; more recently, Gustavo Haical, Contrato de Agência, Editora Revista dos Tribunais, São Paulo, 2012.

of intermediary services corresponds to a compensation or retribution, characterising the contract as *bilateral*, *onerous* and *commutative*. It is also a personal contract. The representation must be operated within a contractually determined territory. Exclusivity is a key element, because the same agent or distributor may not distribute the same or similar products from more than one representee, nor may the representee have more than one agent or distributor for his or her products in the same specified area (Article 711 CC/02).

517. The representee may determine a minimum volume of products to be put on the market, thus obliging the distributor to reach that quota.

518. Nevertheless, the text of the Civil Code entails a number of issues that cause confusion regarding these concepts. The similarity between these kinds of contract and their physical proximity within the statute (being in the same chapter) may lead to confusion with commercial representation; so much so that the Civil Code refers to the application of special legislation, i.e., Law n° 4.886/65 in Article 721 CC/02. Harmonizing the legislation regarding commercial representation and the Civil Code has proven to be very difficult.

III. Difference Between Agency and Distribution[162]

519. The difference between agency and distribution is linked to the subject that has the goods: the distributor has the goods while the agent does not. However, despite the text of the law the phenomenon refers to distribution *lato sensu*. Paula Forgioni[163] classifies the contract as atypical due to the presence of obligations that are typical of other forms of contract.

520. Whenever a service provider is certified as such, the law of commercial representation shall apply (Article 5° of Law n° 4.886/65), which is extremely protective of those who render services habitually and professionally.

521. This law is a legal microsystem, and the new Civil Code only applies subsidiarily. The standards of the code in this respect are of an operative nature.

162. There are numerous books and articles on this subject, we have selected some of the most noteworthy, such as Haical, op. ment., p. 86; Paula Forgioni, Contrato de Distribuição, Revista dos Tribunais, São Paulo, 3rd edition, 2014, p. 76; Roberta Oertel, Le contrat international de Distribution, Concession et Franchise – Comparaison France-Brésil, Bruylant, Droit et Économie, 2016; Ana Carolina Zanetti, Contrato de Distribuição, o inadimplemento recíproco, editora Atlas, São Paulo, 2015, p. 41. Vera Jacob de Fradera, Contrato de Distribuição, in Tratado de Direito Empresarial, Coordenação de Modesto Carvalhosa, vol. IV, Contratos Mercantis, 2ª tiragem, 2016, editora Revista dos Tribunais, São Paulo, 2016, 2ª tiragem, pp. 131–192.

163. V. note 157 *supra*.

Chapter 2. Rental Agreements

§1. Introduction

522. A rental agreement (*locação*, Articles 565–578 CC/02) is a contract in which one party, in exchange for payment, grants the use and fruition of a non-fungible asset to another party. In Brazil, a rental agreement can comprehend movable or immovable property – the latter being subject to special rules.[164]

§2. Characteristics of Rental Agreements

I. Classification

523. Rental agreements are bilateral, consensual, onerous, commutative and impersonal agreements of successive duration or performance. *Bilateral* means that both parties have interdependent obligations; while *consensual* indicates that the agreement of the parties is sufficient for its formation – the delivery of the object of the rental agreement is not necessary to complete the contract. *Onerous* implies that costs are involved, thus distinguishing rental agreements from loan for use agreements (*comodato*). The attribute *impersonal* refers to the fact that the actual individuals who are part of the agreement are not of fundamental importance – each party may transfer its contractual rights to third parties. The *successive duration* or *performance* of the rental agreement indicates that it is not interminable. Its duration is determined in the contract.

II. Legal Nature

524. A rental agreement is a consensual contract and not a real contract. The object of a rental agreement may be non-fungible and non-consumable movable or immovable properties. Fungible assets are objects of loan contracts. The object of a rental agreement, however, may not necessarily be the property of the person offering that object for rent.

525. In some cases, it is possible to rent consumable goods such as certain kinds of decoration products.

526. Regarding rental contracts of movable properties, it is important to highlight the lease contract (*Arrendamento Mercantil*), which is governed by special rules.

164. *See* Carlos Roberto Gonçalves, Direito Civil Brasileiro, Vol III. 3rd edition, São Paulo: Saraiva, 2007; Sílvio de Salvo Venosa, Direito civil: Contratos em Espécie. 9th edition. São Paulo: Atlas, 2009; Venosa, Sílvio de Salvo. Lei do Inquilinato Comentada: doutrina e prática: Lei n° 8.245 from 18 Oct. 1991, 7th edition, São Paulo: Atlas S.A., 2004.

527. The rules of the Brazilian Civil Code apply to all kinds of immovable properties that are not governed by the Tenancy Law (*Lei do Inquilinato*): autonomous parking spaces; parking spaces that are not part of urban residential estates; spaces designed for advertising, such as billboards; flats and apartment hotels; outlet boxes or stores, spaces in trade fairs and exhibition pavilions.

III. Parties

528. The parties in a rental agreement are the landlord, landholder or lessor (*Locador, Senhorio, Arrendador*), and the lessee, tenant or leaseholder (*Locatário, Inquilino, Arrendatário*).

IV. Rent

529. The rent (*aluguel*) is the price paid for the use of an asset, such as a house, while a lease (*arrendamento*) is the price paid for the use and exploitation, such as the lease of a farm or ranch.

530. The rent represents the compensation or the price paid for the use of the object rented. It is not always a sum of money; the parties may agree on other forms of compensation.

V. Obligations of the Lessor and the Lessee

531. The rules of the Brazilian Civil Code on this topic are to be found in Articles 566, 567, 568, 569 and 570.

532. A rental agreement cannot be perpetual; it must have a determined or determinable duration – *see* Articles 573 (not applicable to urban rentals), 574 and 575 CC/02.

VI. Building Rentals

533. The Brazilian Civil Code distinguishes urban properties (*imóvel urbano*) from rural properties (*imóvel rústico*), without providing their specific definitions. The legal literature has developed some criteria for classification.

534. The location criterion establishes that estates located in the city area are urban properties and estates located in the countryside are rural properties. The Brazilian Civil Code modified by the Tenancy Law governs urban properties; rural properties are regulated by the Land Statute (*Estatuto da Terra*) (Articles 92 et seq., Law n° 4.504 from 30 November 1964).

535. In urban property rentals, social aspects, emergency solutions, the protection of current tenants through rent control, prohibition of eviction, facilitation of home ownership through the provision of long-term loans with below-market interest rates are taken into account. Rural property rentals include factors that are typical of country life and are imposed by independent regulations, such as the issues involving usury and the abuse of rights by landowners in relation to rural lessees.

536. Commercial rental entails special protection in relation to goodwill, which prevents eviction of the tenant. This includes the prevention of the unjust enrichment by the landlord due to appreciation of the property resulting from the tenant's work.

§3. Conclusion

537. The legislation on rentals provided by the Brazilian Civil Code has been modified by emergency laws such as the Commercial Tenancy Law (*Lei de Luvas*), the Tenancy Law (*Lei do Inquilinato*) for residential tenancy and Land Statute (*Estatuto da Terra*) for rural tenancy.

538. The former Brazilian Civil Code from 1916 was liberal and capitalist; it regulated the relationship between landlord and tenant differently. There was broad freedom of contract concerning the fixation of the rent, duration, conditions of the rental, etc. Nowadays, the social aspects play a major role in the legislation of this field.[165]

165. *See* Caio Mário da Silva Pereira, Instituições de Direito Civil, vol. III. Forense: Rio de Janeiro, 14th edition, pp. 229–270.

Chapter 3. Gambling and Wagering

§1. Introduction

539. Contracts on gambling (*jogo*) and wagering (*aposta*) are governed by Articles 814–817 in the Civil Code, integrating a peculiar kind of obligation – natural obligation (*obrigação natural*). The only legal effect of natural obligation is non-repetition. This effect is common to lawful and unlawful games.

540. According to Sálvio Venosa,[166] in a *gambling* contract, two or more parties oblige themselves to pay a certain amount of money or something other than money to the party that wins in an intellectual or physical activity.

541. The same author defines a *wagering* contract as one by which two or more parties promise an equivalent sum for the opinion on a given subject, a natural fact or acts of third parties.

§2. Characteristics of Gambling and Wagering Contracts

542. Games and wagers have always existed in society. While many of their characteristics have remained unchanged, certain aspects have been updated, and today many forms of games and wagers are regulated by law.

543. The first observation to be made is that games and wagers are bilateral, onerous, random contracts, involving a natural obligation.

544. It should be noted that some forms of gambling and wagering are prohibited, and therefore any claims would not be legally recognized and cannot be pursued in the court of law. However, there are others that, because they are governed by law, are allowed and constitute civil obligations, i.e., they entail debts and liability, and, as a result, have recourse.

§3. Types of Gambles

545. According to the doctrine, gambles and wagers may be legal (allowed by law), lawful (tolerated) or illegal (forbidden).

546. With regards to permitted and/or prohibited gambles, and taking into account the moral aspects of such obligations, Brazilian law determines that obligations resulting from gambling and wagering do not require to be fulfilled, but a party that paid an amount voluntarily cannot reclaim it, unless it was won by fraud, the loser is under age or declared incapable (Article 814 CC/02). This provision

166. Direito Civil, Contratos em espécie, 9th edition, 2009, Editora Atlas, São Paulo, p. 391.

extends to any contract that covers recognition, novation or guarantee of the gambling debt. However, the resulting nullity cannot harm third parties in good faith. The provision does not apply to forms of gambling and wagering that are legally allowed, such as the state lottery.

547. Awards or promises offered to the winner in a competition of a sporting, intellectual or artistic nature are also exceptions, provided that the parties concerned comply with legal or regulatory requirements.

548. Along the same line of reasoning, the legislator prohibits the demand of repayment of amounts borrowed for the purposes of gambling or wagering in the act of wagering or gambling (Article 815 CC/02).

549. However, borrowing money to pay off wagering debts is not prohibited and the debtor must repay any such loan to the lender.

550. In Brazil, games like tennis, for example, are deemed lawful, in the same way as those involving intellectual skill, like chess, are legally accepted. There are, however, games in which luck is the factor that determines who will be the winner and the loser. These types of games are prohibited because their only goal is economic, with the advantage of some and the disadvantage of many, such as roulette. The purpose is profit or gain without work, intelligence or skill. The Law of Criminal Offenses (*Lei das Contravenções Penais*), in Article 50, prohibits these types of games. This same law prohibits betting on horse races outside the racetrack. However, decree n° 50.776/61 allows clubs, etc. to practise lawful games such as playing cards within the environs of their premises.

551. Article 817 CC/02 regulates matters related to raffles (*sorteio*): a raffle is a sharing system or transaction process that may be used to settle questions or to distribute common things among certain people. The purpose of the raffle is to settle an impasse, a related difficulty. Under the terms of Article 817 CC/02, the interested parties who face an impasse may resolve it by holding a raffle. It is equivalent to a shared system or a transaction process.

552. The raffle may have its form provided for in the law, be chosen by the parties or determined by a judge.

Chapter 4. Sale of Goods

§1. Introduction

553. The purchase and sale agreement (*contrato de compra e venda*) is the oldest, the most important and the most complex contract.

554. According to the Brazilian Civil Code, one of the parties in a purchase and sale contract agrees to transfer the dominium (property) of a certain thing, while the other party agrees to pay the price in money.[167]

555. Reasons related to legal security and predictability determine the choice of the property transmission system.[168]

556. The Brazilian system of property transfer has its roots in Roman law and is also inspired by German law and its *Pandektenrecht*, i.e., Digest. There are two means or models of transferring property: the causal and the abstract model.

557. The French system is the best example of the causal model, in which the contract transfers the property. German law constitutes an example of the abstract model. In German law,[169] there is a distinction between the sales contract, which generates obligations, the *Kaufvertrag*, and the *abstract act*, which operates the transfer of the property, *Übereignung*.

558. These two acts are independent of one another; if the first act is faulty, the second one will not be contaminated by its vice. Due to this separation, the *Trennungsprinzip,* the second act is considered *abstrait.*[170]

559. The Brazilian legislator partially adopted the German model. Like the Germans, the Brazilian legislators of the Codes from 1916 and 2002 chose a model inspired by Roman law and the Digest (*Pandekten*).

560. Nevertheless, Brazilian law chose a very peculiar system to transfer goods:[171] the contract of purchase and sale is elaborated on two levels. The first level relates to the obligation relationship, i.e., by the contract, the parties agree to purchase and to sell something for a sum of money. The buyer pays the price, but

167. Article 481 CC/02.
168. Rodolfo Sacco, Le Transfert de la Propriété des Choses Mobilières Déterminées par Acte entre Vifs en Droit Comparé. Rivista di Diritto Civile, Milano, n. 4, 1979, pp. 442–447. About the same subject see the remarkable article of Franco Ferrari, Abstraktionsprinzip, Traditionsprinzip e Consensualismo nel Transferimento di Beni Mobili. Una Superabile Divaricazione? Rivista de Diritto Civile, Milano, n. 6, 1993, pp. 729–757.
169. Otto Palandt. Bürgerliches Gesetzbuch. 52nd edition, Munich: C.H. Beck, 1988.
170. Le Droit Allemand, Michel Pedamon, Col. Que sais-je? PUF, Paris, 1985, pp. 42–43; Iacyr de Aguilar Vieira, Compra e Venda e a Transferência da Propriedade, Modelos Causais e Abstratos Revista dos Tribunais, São Paulo: RT v. 88, n. 765 (July 1999) pp. 59–77.
171. *See* Clóvis do Couto e Silva, A Obrigação como Processo. São Paulo: Bushastky, 1986.

he or she is not the owner until the seller performs the transfer (*tradition*, if the thing is movable). When the object of the contract is real estate, the transfer must be recorded in the *Estate Register*. In contrast to the German model, in Brazilian law, the separation of the levels is relative, i.e., a problem at the obligation level affects the second level and the transfers cannot be performed. Registration ensures the transfer of the property with *erga omnes* effects. One of the most relevant consequences of registration is the legal security ensuing from it. The whole community, for example, the creditors of both parties, is aware of the transaction.[172]

561. Among the types of purchase and sale agreements there are: agreements to buy and sell property and assets (urban and rural); as well as tangible and intangible things (in case of intangible things the term '*cessão*' – assignment – applies); and national, international, and transnational, as well as civil and commercial agreements. Their importance for trade in general is notable since they are key to ensuring the circulation of goods.

562. Historically, the purchase and sale agreement was a response to the needs arising from the circulation of wealth, which obliged men to exchange goods for other goods or services. It led to the emergence of a currency, which resulted in a common denominator of trade, and increasing commerce until the acts of buying and selling became distinguished from those of exchange and barter.

563. A purchase and sale contract is bilateral (the seller must deliver the goods and the buyer must pay the price); consensual (it depends on the agreement of wills); commutative (the price and value of services or goods should correspond) or, exceptionally, random, when there is uncertainty as to the existence of one of the benefits, for example, merchandise located in the basement of a ship that may have sunk or a future harvest that may or may not take place, or as to their values.

564. If the purpose of the transfer is only the use of the assets, the contract will be a renting or loan contract rather than a purchase and sale agreement. If there is no price to pay, the contract is a donation.

§2. Essential Elements of the Sale of Goods

565. The essential elements of the sale of goods are the object, the price and consent.

566. The object (*objeto*) can be any assets, unless it is inalienable (family assets, mortgaged property, assets with clauses which forbid alienation, liens arising from

172. V. Leonardo Brandelli, 'Abstração e Causalidade entre o plano real e o obrigacional e as espécies registrais imobiliárias', Revista de Direito Imobiliário, vol. 79, 1938, Editora Revista dos Tribunais, São Paulo, pp. 85–124, jul./dec. 2015.

contracts or wills, usufruct, right of succession of a living person). Thus, corporeal things and intangible assets, securities, shares, loans, future things and unrelated things may be object of sale agreements.

567. The price (*preço*) is fixed in cash, must be determined or determinable, and may depend on values quoted on the Stock Exchange on the day of delivery of the goods (Article 486 CC/02), or fixed by a third party (Article 485 CC/02). However, the price cannot depend on the will of one party only, since such behaviour is forbidden by law (Article 489 CC/02).

568. In order to have consent (*consenso*) among the parties, general legal capacity possibly requiring assistance (*assistência*) or representation (*representação*) is essential. There are, however, cases in which the law forbids a certain person to trade due to a lack of legitimacy, e.g., a bankrupted person. There may be a sale without the owner's consent, e.g., a judicial auction.

569. Refusal to supply certain goods is a violation of the Popular Economy Law (*Lei de Crimes contra a Economia Popular*, Law n° 1.521 from 26 December 1951, Article 2).

570. The form of purchase and sale agreements is generally free, being solemn only for the transfer of real estate property (*see* Articles 107[173] and 108[174] CC/02).

§3. Rights and Duties of the Parties in the Sale of Goods

571. The parties in the sale of goods have the duty to deliver the goods and respectively the right to receive the price (Article 491 CC/02). The delivery of goods is due upon receiving the price when the sale is in plain sight (Articles 491 and 495 CC/02). If the seller cannot deliver the goods, the buyer is not obliged to pay the price.

572. Under Article 495 CC/02, the seller has the right to require the buyer to pay a deposit as a guarantee for the payment of the total price, even if the buyer has already become insolvent. At the same time, the buyer has the right to refuse goods sold by sample (Article 484 CC/02). Regardless of the sale, he or she cannot, however, reject all the purchased goods as a whole, although some of them have a defect (Article 503 CC/02). According to Article 500 CC/02, in a sale *ad mensuram* the solutions of the law apply when there is a missing part of the amounts contracted.

173. The validity of a declaration of will does not depend on any special form, unless the law expressly requires it.

174. Article 108 CC. Unless otherwise specified by law, the public deed is essential for the validity of legal transactions which aim to establish, transfer, modify or waive real estate property worth more than thirty times the highest minimum wage in the country.

§4. Secondary or Natural Elements of the Purchase and Sale Agreement

573. Secondary or natural elements are presumed to exist in the purchase and sale, unless otherwise agreed by the parties. These are duties whose source is the supplementary law. The seller is liable in the event of foreclosure or in case of a redhibitory defect or vice (*vícios redibitorios*). Another example is the liability for the risks of goods, which means that until the transfer to the buyer, the seller is liable for any damages (Article 492 CC/02). The buyer, however, is liable for the damages resulting from the counting or marking of goods and for all damages that occur after the tradition, or independently of it, since the sold object has been made available to the purchaser who is in default to receive it.

§5. Basic and Essential Obligations in Certain Types of Sale

574. In the Sale of Real Estate, the seller must present clearance certificates and prove in writing the absence of tax debts with the Federal, State and County and Social Security.

575. In the Sale of Goods in Condominium, there are pre-emptive rights of the shareholders in the sale of common parts.

576. The Sale by Sample is intended to save time and money and allow for goods to be carried from afar. However, this type of agreement may entail risks, because the sample can, for instance, be miniaturized. The seller guarantees the buyer that the goods sold have the same qualities as the presented sample (Article 484 CC/02; Article 26 CDC). Under the Civil Code, when there is lack of conformity, the contract is voidable.

577. In an *ad corpus* Sale, a property is sold as a certain and determined asset, as a whole, requiring a descriptive reference to the dimensions (Article 500 CC/02). The law does not admit claims for recalculating the area, for the termination of the contract or for a price reduction.

578. In *ad mensuram* Sales (Article 500 CC/02), the dimensions of the property are essential to define the price (per metre, or per kilo, for example) and to fulfil the objective of the legal transaction. If the dimensions of the property do not match those measurements contained in the public deed, the buyer has the right to demand the complementation of the area (*actio ex empto*), based on the non-performance of the contract. If this is not possible, the law offers two alternatives: the annulment of the contract (*actio redhibitoria*) or a proportional reduction in the price *(actio quanti minoris*).

§6. Expenses in the Sale of Goods

579. Under Article 490 CC/02, the burden for transfer expenses, e.g., deeds, should be paid by the seller, while transfer taxes should be paid by the buyer. However, such rules can be set aside by the parties.

580. In commercial contracts, there is the FOB price (free on board) when all the expenses are the responsibility of the buyer, while with CIF (Cost, Insurance and Freight) the insurance and freight are the responsibility of the seller.

581. Article 491 CC/02 regulates cash sales. In such situations, the seller is not obliged to deliver the good/s before receiving the payment.

582. In 1990, the Consumer Protection Code (Law n° 8.078) entered into force and provoked relevant modifications concerning the concept of purchase and sale agreements. According to this law, the consumers – a category of persons – were considered uneven and hypo-sufficient compared to a seller, a manufacturer or an importer. For this reason, the Consumer Protection Code created new rules to regulate this special kind of relationship, granting particular protection to the consumer.

583. Consequently, some contracts that were previously considered civil contracts are now subject to different regulations, for example, the sale of goods. If two equal parties (two businessmen, or a businessman and a corporation) agree on a sale, it is regulated by the Civil Code; however, if the sales contract is formed between a consumer and a store, the consumer law will regulate this purchase and sale.

584. When the Consumer Protection Code entered into force, the former Civil Code from 1916 was still in force, and it was considered an obsolete law by many scholars. For this reason, the Consumer Protection Code appeared to be a modern codification (inspired by the European Directive 85/374/CEE from 25 July 1985), and, prior to the publication of the current Civil Code, it was applied as an alternative to the *old* Civil Code. Nevertheless, the present authors, among others, consider this position erroneous, because the nature of the consumer law is very different from that of the Civil Code. The rules of the latter are addressed to equal entities that are unprotected by the Consumer Protection Code, whose recipients are considered vulnerable.

585. Today, almost thirty years after the publication of the Civil Code, we can note that a new conception of the importance of this code has been constructed.

Chapter 5. Works Contracts

§1. Introduction

586. The subject of hiring work or services is studied within the general framework of the lease because of its historical origins. As *per* its definition, a works contract (*empreitada*) is an agreement by which one undertakes to do certain work for others for payment.[175]

587. It originated in Roman law, where the *locatio operis faciendi* had its origin in the *locatio-conductio.*

588. The word 'work', in its definition, has the sense of result to be obtained by the activity or work, such as the production or modification of things, the transport of persons or goods, carrying out scientific work or the creation of artistic material or immaterial work. However, not all of these activities constitute an undertaking in Brazilian law.

589. The 'work' does not need to be an exclusive product of the party bound to execute it, unless the contract was executed *intuitu personae*. Generally, any person may undertake to perform certain work that does not require any further organization of the means of production. It is, in itself, sufficient to promise the result of the work.

§2. Parties to Works Contracts

590. The contractor (*empreiteiro*) performs or is responsible for the performance of the work; he/she is the debtor of the work; the creditor of the payment. The developer (*comitente*) is the one who orders the performance and pays the price; he/she is creditor of the work; the debtor of the payment.

591. The contract can have its object performed in instalments or in benefits arising from certain services.

§3. Observations about the Similarities Between Works, Purchase and Sale and Employment Contracts

592. When the contractor provides the materials for the work, the works contract is similar to the purchase and sale contract. However, if the most important element of the contract is the work ordered, the contract will be a works contract.

175. Arnoldo Wald, Contratos, op. ment., p. 404.

593. Works contracts sometimes seem similar to employment contracts, as both involve the professional activity of a person. However, the two types of contracts are different because they are subject to two different legal regimes.

594. Roman law distinguished the *locatio operarum* (duty to provide services) from the *locatio operis faciendi* (promise to do something). There is considerable doctrinal debate regarding the legal nature of works contracts. The essential difference from an employment contract lies in the fact that the latter is based on the existence of a relationship of subordination, while the parties in works contracts are autonomous.

595. In addition, works contracts share similarities with supply agreements, in which there is also the regular rendering of services. The difference lies in the quality of the benefit. In works contracts, while the promise of a finished job is implicit, the execution of the work is the most important element. In supply agreements, however, the predominant aspect is the production of an asset, or the possibility of its use for the proposed purpose, for which the work is a subsidiary or preparatory element. In short, in works contracts, the most important element is the *facere (doing it)*; while in supply agreements is the *dare (delivering the finished object).*

§4. Characteristic Features of Works Contracts

596. Works contracts are bilateral; onerous; simply consensual; usually of singular performance; and, occasionally, of long duration.

597. The fact that it is onerous is essential to the contract, for it cannot be free. The price is the differentiating element of the contract in relation to the mandate and the donation.

598. It is formed by the mere consent of both parties and, generally, does not require any special form. However, sometimes a form is required, for example, the construction of a building should be a contract executed in writing, due to the need to clearly specify details, leaving no room for doubt. It is still not solemn. A works contract usually entails a single execution, but the contractor may undertake to produce the work that is performed repeatedly several times in independent units. This aspect does not attribute any employment or supply characteristics to works contracts.

§5. Types of Works Contracts

I. Works Contract *of Labour*

599. In a 'works contract *of labour*' (*empreitada de lavor*), the contractor only contributes labour, i.e., he or she provides labour using materials provided by the developer or commissioned by the developer from third parties. Works contracts *of labour* are similar to services since other people's labour is used. However, the difference lies in the purpose of the contracts. In works contracts, a party is hired to carry out the work; in the service lease, a party hires the employee's labour. Payment is also different: in works contracts, the contractor is paid for the result; while in employment contracts, the employee is paid for his or her efforts, regardless of the outcome. Another difference is that in works contracts, the contractor is relatively autonomous, whereas in employment contracts, there is no autonomy, unless it is technical work.

II. Works Contract

600. In a *mixed* works contract (*empreitada mista*), the contractor provides both labour and the necessary materials. In this setting, works contracts are similar to the purchase and sale of future things

III. Works Contracts for a Fixed Price

601. Works Contracts can also be for a fixed price, when the fee is fixed in advance; per unit or custom, when the price is established per dimensions of construction; or by administration, when material expenses are borne by the developer and a percentage is paid to the contractor for his work.

602. The obligations of the contractor and the developer are provided in Articles 615, 617, 618, and 619 CC/02.

§6. Works Contract Risks

603. The law does not allow the readjustment of fixed-price contracts, but case law has established the understanding to accept the adjustment based on the *rebus sic stantibus* clause and unpredictability theory.

604. The non-receipt of the work qualifies as a lack of performance by the developer.

605. Termination of the contract occurs by means of completion of the work and payment of the price. Other causes of termination include force majeure, death of the contractor in an *intuitu personae* contract, termination of the contract due to the extinction of its object, and expropriation of the property.

§7. Liability for the Solidity of the Works

606. Under Article 618 CC/02, the contractor of materials and work for buildings or other significant constructions will be liable during the irreducible period of

5 years for the solidity, strength and safety of the construction, as well as the materials and soil issues. However, the rights established in this article shall decay if the developer does not bring an action against the contractor within the period of 180 days following the onset of vice or defect.

607. Contractors of materials are liable for the price thereof acquired from third parties and for the payment of labour and damages caused to third parties.

608. It is allowed to have both individual and joint liability between the contractor and developer, by which the developer is at fault in choosing *(in eligendo)* or overseeing *(in vigilando)* in relation to the contractor.

§8. CONCLUSION

609. The rules contained in the Civil Code on works contracts govern only a few situations in daily life. The vast majority of works contracts are regulated by the Consumer Protection Code, because consumers are the ones who generally make use of works contracts and are often economically hypo-sufficient before contractors.

Chapter 6. Leasing

§1. Introduction

610. Leasing (*arrendamento*) is one of the most important contracts in Brazil and it extensively contributes to the country's economic development.

611. It originated from North America and was legally regulated in Brazil a few decades ago, in the 1970s, through Law n° 6.099/74 and Resolution no. 351/75, which was edited with the exclusive goal of dealing with the lease only for tax purposes.

612. Initially, national legislators restricted the use of leasing to corporations. It was only in 1983, by virtue of Law n° 7.132/83, which altered the sole paragraph of Law n° 6.099/74, that the use of leasing also became available to individuals. The law determines that leasing is a legal transaction between a corporation, acting as lessor, and individuals or other corporations, acting as lessee, the object of which is the leasing of goods acquired by the lessor, according to specifications determined by the lessee and for the latter's use.

613. Arnold Wald defines the lease contract as a mixed contract, by which a lessor (corporation) acquires and then rents a movable or immovable good to someone else (individual or corporation) to use it for the long or medium term, while the acquisition of the good for the residual value is optional to the lessee.[176]

614. We would also like to quote Silvio Venosa's definition, for whom lease is the contract by which an agent, intending to use a movable or immovable good, makes a financial or specialized institution to acquire it, so as to rent that good later for a certain period, giving the agent the option to finally return the good, to renew the contract, or to acquire the good for the established residual value.[177]

615. Still, according to the same author, the essence of the transaction, under the legislation, is a financial operation to procure a fixed asset. The lessor company, subject to the Central Bank's control and monitoring, is the operation's intermediary, obtaining resources from the market and passing them on through leasing. This way, in our legal system, the lessor must necessarily be a corporation integrated into the financial system. The established residual value is often symbolic and inferior to the market price. The establishment of a residual value is characteristic of finance leasing, which is the most widely used form of leasing. Through this clause, the parties fix, at that moment, the value the good shall have by the end of the leasing period. In the financial world, this stipulation is called 'guaranteed residual value' (*valor residual em garantia*).

---

176. Wald, Arnold. Obrigações e Contratos, Editora Saraiva, São Paulo, 2004, 16th edition, pp. 673 et seq.

177. Venosa, Silvio. Direito Civil, Contratos em Espécie, Editora Atlas, São Paulo, 2009, 9th edition, pp. 562 et seq.

616. The Brazilian Civil Code from 2002 did not foresee the lease contract among the range of nominate contracts, despite it having been used for years by national companies.[178]

617. There are two relevant aspects to be considered on this matter. First, the circulation of legal juridical models in Brazil's social, economic and legal settings is an undeniable fact. For many years, Brazil has imported European and North American legal models. Second, in an as-yet-restricted manner, the legislators of the 2002 Civil Code have recognized the principle of private autonomy in Article 425 stating that the parties are allowed to stipulate innominate contracts, as longs as the general rules established by this Code are observed.

618. Leasing is a bilateral, consensual, onerous and commutative contract, which may only be performed in written form.

619. As in its country of origin, the US, and in other countries that have adopted it, leasing presents itself in many shapes, depending on the desired goals of both parties.

§2. Types of Leasing

620. In the following paragraphs, we will briefly introduce some of the forms of leasing: traditional leasing, leaseback, self-leasing, operating leasing, and dummy corporations.

621. Traditional leasing, also called *finance leasing* (*leasing tradicional ou financeiro*) involves three parties, a lessee or leaseholder, a lessor and a supplier.

622. Leaseback or *Sale and Leaseback* operates in a similar way to finance leasing, except for the fact that there is no supplier, since the object of the contract integrates the assets of the lessor company.

623. Relating to this matter, Article 9 of Law n° 6.099/74 states that lease operations arranged with the seller of the good or with corporations associated to the seller, by means of any of the relationships foreseen by Article 2 of this law, will also be able to be performed by financial institutions expressly authorized by the National Monetary Council, who shall establish the conditions to perform the operations foreseen in this article (as written in Law n° 7.132 from 1983).

624. Operating Leasing (*leasing operacional*) contains neither an obligatory option clause nor is there any intervention by a financial institution. This makes it much easier to close an operating lease, since manufacturers or suppliers promote it.

---

178. For further information on leasing's innominate status, *see* Mauro Bussani, I Contratti Nuovi, Giuffrè Editore, Milano, 1989, pp. 31 et seq.

625. *Operating and Maintenance Leasing* is a type of lease where, besides a common lease operation, the lessee also hires technical assistance or maintenance for the material discussed in the agreement.

626. In addition, a *Leasing Broker* or rather *leasing agent* is a lessor who acts as a sort of intermediary, receiving a commission for services rendered.

627. A *Dummy Corporation* or *Société de Paille* in France was created to act as an intermediary between lessee and investors. It is managed by a trustee, nominated by the investors themselves, to whom the rents owed by the lessees are paid.

628. Professor Arnoldo Wald[179] calls attention to an important aspect of the lease contract in Brazil, namely *para-financial agencies*. These agencies do not conduct typical financial activities, but regarding specific aspects are subject to control by Brazil's Central Bank. Lease operations are thus regulated, and the lessor companies are controlled and monitored by the Central Bank.

629. Another important aspect of the use of leasing in Brazil is the possible application of the Consumer Protection Code to the lessees. This code clearly defines the consumer as the party who acquires the good for his or her own use. However, after much hesitation, case law has been admitting the application of the Consumer Protection Code in certain aspects of the contract, such as interest rates and leasing price readjustment, arguing that the lease contract is an adhesion contract and hence would be subject to the Consumer Protection Code. The present authors understand that this argument has no basis, since contracts between equals may be written in the shape of General Conditions of Contracts or by adherence.

630. As for the positive aspects and advantages of leasing, we, once again, refer to Arnoldo Wald,[180] who considers it an important factor for increasing productivity, since it permits the substitution of used or obsolete equipment for new ones. Furthermore, the use of leasing saves working capital, since by operating in this area, companies offer positions to various professional categories (engineers, lawyers, economists, etc.), and the government collects taxes thanks to this activity.

631. Finally, we present some considerations on the extinguishment of the lease contract. Like any contract, the lease contract has a beginning, a development and an end, since the duration of the contract is sometimes indeterminate. However, unforeseen difficulties may affect the duration: for example, the death of the lessee, if the contract is stipulated *intuitu personae*; the occurrence of force majeure; or even the loss or destruction of the good – the object of the lease– although such goods are normally insured. Non-compliance with the agreement by one of the parties provokes its termination.

179. Op., p. 570.
180. Op. mentioned pp. 573 and 574.

Chapter 7. Settlements

632. Some codes consider settlement (*transação*) a means of extinguishing obligations; however, it should be classified as a kind of contract. Despite being understood as a form of payment, settlement has the authentic nature of a contract.

633. Settlement is defined by Orlando Gomes[181] as a contract by which, through mutual concessions, interested parties prevent or terminate a dispute, eliminating the uncertainty of a legal relationship.[182]

634. The first point to be noted in relation to settlement refers to the type of dispute that can be prevented or terminated: *only those related to private equity claims* (Article 841 CC/02).

§1. Settlement Form

635. The transaction shall be done by means of a public deed for the obligations that the law determines, or by private agreement when allowed. If it concerns rights which are challenged in court, it shall be by deed or by documents in the lawsuit, signed by both parties and approved by the judge.

I. Settlement Requirement

636. The requirement for a settlement is uncertainty of a legal relationship, which is eliminated contractually through mutual concessions.

II. Settlement Types

637. The settlement can be preventive or terminative. Thus, Article 840 CC/02 provides that it is permissible for interested parties to prevent or terminate their disputes through mutual concessions.

638. The first type aims at preventing a dispute by eliminating a situation of uncertainty through mutual concessions. According to Orlando Gomes,[183] justice is slow in Brazil, hence this type of settlement is often used to avoid wasting time awaiting a judicial decision. It is not so much the legal process itself that is to be avoided, but rather the loss of time due to the conditions prevailing in the Brazilian Judiciary.

---

181. Contratos, Editora Forense, 12ª edição, pp. 499 et seq.
182. Some aspects of this contract have been discussed by scholars like Arnoldo WALD, in Obrigações e Contratos, op.cit., pp. 122 and seq.
183. Contratos, already mentioned, p. 500.

639. The second type, the terminative settlement, as the name suggests, puts an end to a legal dispute by making mutual concessions.

640. According to the provisions of the 2002 Civil Code, a dispute ended by settlement can be terminated first by a document in the lawsuit as executed by both parties, second by public deed, for obligations that the law requires; and third by a private agreement when admitted.

641. However, regardless of the form adopted in the agreement, any terminative settlement will always require the approval of a judge.

642. Given this characteristic, this agreement is called a 'court settlement' (*transação judicial*), while, at the same time, it is both a judicial act and a civil act.

III. Nullity of the Settlement

643. Under Article 848 CC/02, if any of the settlement terms are declared null and void, the settlement shall be null and void.

IV. Voidability of the Settlement

644. Under Article 849 CC/02, a settlement is voidable only in the case of fraud, coercion or critical error as to the person or controversial thing. A settlement is not cancelled by error of law on the issues that were the subject of controversy between the parties. It is also voidable if none of the parties was aware of it, or if, by a title that was discovered later, it appears that none of them had any right regarding the object of settlement (Article 850 CC/02).

§2. Interpretation of Legal Settlement and Relevant Distinctions

645. Settlement shall be interpreted restrictively, because it cannot transmit rights but only declare or recognize rights (Article 843 CC/02).

I. Settlement Scope

646. According to Article 844 CC/02, a settlement shall not provide any advantage or cause any prejudice except to those who intervened in it, even if it regards an indivisible asset.

647. If the creditor and the debtor agree on a settlement, the guarantor is relieved. If it is reached between one of the joint creditors and the debtor, it extinguishes the obligation of the debtor before all other creditors. If the settlement is completed by one of the joint debtors and their creditor, it extinguishes the obligation of all the debtors before the creditor.

II. Settlement and Eviction

648. Under Article 845 CC/02, in the case the thing that caused the transaction is evicted (the loss of the thing waived by one of the parties to a third party, whose right prevailed by court decision), the obligation that is extinguished by the transaction is not reinstated. He who lost the goods to third party (*evicto*), will have the right to compensation.

III. Settlement and Criminal Offence

649. According to Article 846 CC/02, a settlement concerning obligations arising from criminal activities does not extinguish the State's right to undertake criminal proceedings if the fact that gave rise to the obligation (e.g., compensation) was criminal.

650. Under Article 847 CC/02, a conventional penalty in the settlement is permissible. When a transaction involves several independent disputed rights, the fact that one does not prevail shall not prejudice any other.

Chapter 8. Suretyship

§1. Introduction

651. Suretyship (*fiança*) is a personal, accessory, subsidiary guarantee under Article 818 of the Brazilian Civil Code.[184] Article 818 CC/02 describes the suretyship contract as a contract by which a person (the guarantor) guarantees the creditor to perform an obligation of the debtor, in case he or she fails to do so.

652. It is a unilateral contract because only the guarantor undertakes obligations, unless he or she receives some kind of compensation – in such case, the suretyship will be turned into an insurance guarantee.

653. Suretyship is important because it serves as a guarantee in general trade. There is some controversy in relation to both marriage and stable relationships (*união estável*) regarding the validity of surety without marital authorization (*outorga uxória* or rather *marital*). Traditionally, Brazilian law required the consent of such a partner when granting guarantee. However, since the Code from 2002, this has no longer been mandatory. This fact may cause problems when one of the partners grants a guarantee involving more than his or her own assets without consulting the other partner. This issue has not yet been definitely decided in Brazilian jurisprudence.

654. Historically, suretyship has been recognized since antiquity, especially by the Romans: one of the oldest forms of suretyship was the Roman *sponsio*.

§2. Elements of Suretyship Contract

655. As a personal guarantee, in case of non-performance of the main obligation by the debtor, the assets of the guarantor will cover the debt. The guarantor will then be entitled to subrogation of the creditor's rights in the amount paid.

656. The guarantor has two main rights: right of order and right of division.

657. 'Right of order' means that the guarantor may require that the debtor's assets be used to pay the debt first. However, this right does not exist if the guarantor expressly waives it in the conclusion of the suretyship agreement or declares himself as joint debtor or primary obligor. Such clauses are null and void when the agreement concerns consumer relationships.

184. *See* Gildo dos Santos, 'A Fiança', in O Novo Código Civil, Estudos em Homenagem ao Prof. Miguel Reale, Orgs. Domingos Franciulli Netto, Gilmar Ferreira Mendes, Ives Gandra Martins, Editora LTr, São Paulo, 2003, p. 747.

658. Right of division refers to the fact that when more than one guarantor is involved in the suretyship agreement, it is possible to determine the part or proportion of the debt for which each one is responsible, as stated in Article 831 CC/02. This division should be expressed in the suretyship agreement; otherwise, the co-guarantors will be considered joint debtors. Moreover, the guarantor's obligations are transmitted to his or her heirs. However, the suretyship obligation is limited to the date of the guarantor's death and cannot exceed the amount of the inheritance (Article 836 CC/02).

659. According to Articles 837–839 of the Brazilian Civil Code, the suretyship agreement terminates in case of the fulfilment of the guaranteed obligation by the debtor; the death of the guarantor; or a declaration of invalidity of the suretyship agreement.

§3. Conclusion

660. Suretyship is a unilateral contract; obligations being undertaken only by the guarantor. For some authors, it is an imperfect bilateral agreement because the guarantor is entitled to subrogation of the creditor's rights in the amount paid.

661. Furthermore, it is a non-onerous contract in the field of civil law; the guarantee is provided selflessly. However, regarding bank and commercial suretyship, the guarantor may receive monetary compensation. In the field of civil law, any payment for a suretyship is considered an unlawful transaction.

662. It is *intuitu personae*, consensual and formal contract. Commercial suretyship (*Fiança Mercantil*) was revoked by the Brazilian Civil Code from 2002.

Chapter 9. Pledge (*Pignus*)

§1. Introduction

663. The pledge (*penhor*) is governed by Articles 1.431–1.472 of the Brazilian Civil Code. It concerns guarantees that might be of a personal or a real nature – the latter being subdivided into real rights *in* guarantee and real rights *of* guarantee (*direitos reais em garantia e direitos reais de garantia*).

664. The pledge contract is an important and very old type of contract that plays an important role in the market, especially in periods of economic crisis during which people may need loans but do not have real estate property to guarantee the credit. Nowadays, contrary to the old aphorism that says immovable goods are of greater value than movable goods (*res mobilis vilis et mobilium est vilis possession)*, the importance of movables is widely acknowledged.

665. In the words of Darcy Bessone, 'the guarantee of credit, so connected to economic life and, in a certain way, associated to ethical notions, demands updated techniques from the law'.[185]

666. The pledge contract is related to different areas of law: the Law of Obligations, Property Law, Contract Law and also Commercial Law, which are included in the Brazilian Civil Code from 2002.[186]

667. As highlighted by Alexandre Liquidato[187] in his as yet unpublished dissertation, the pledge contract is 'the legal transaction, that grants effectiveness to the real right of pledge, (…) generating obligations and real rights. (…) Studying the pledge is analysing a multilateral legal relationship from both Contract Law and Property Law, through rights exercised erga omnes, that have equal importance and value'.

668. A pledge is a real right of guarantee, according to which the debtor hands a movable asset to the creditor in guarantee of payment.

669. At first glance, the pledge seems to be a simple contract, but it has a complex structure and can present very diverse forms such as the agricultural pledge (*penhor agrícola*) that exempts the delivery of a movable asset to the creditor.

---

185. Da Compra e Venda: promessa; reserva de domínio & alienação em garantia, Editora Saraiva, 1995, São Paulo, p. 05.
186. Some authors who wrote about this subject: Caio Mário da Silva Pereira, Instituições de direito civil: direitos reais. 19th edition, Rio de Janeiro: Forense, 2012, v. 05; Sílvio Rodrigues. Direito civil: direito das coisas. 28th edition, São Paulo: Saraiva, 2007, v. 05; Flávio Tartuce, Manual de direito civil. Rio de Janeiro: Forense; São Paulo: Método, 2011; Silvio Venosa, Código civil interpretado. 2nd edition, São Paulo: Atlas, 2011; Silvio Venosa, Direito Civil: direito reais, 7th edition, São Paulo, Atlas, 2007, v. 05; Arnold Wald, Direito das coisas, 11th edition, São Paulo: Saraiva, 2002.
187. O Contrato de Penhor, Universidade de São Paulo, São Paulo, 2012, p. 08.

According to the Brazilian system, the following are forms of pledge: rural, agricultural, livestock, industrial and commercial pledge, as well as bond and vehicle pledge.

670. The pledge can derive from law (legal pledge) or from the agreement of the parties (conventional pledge) – the latter being more common. The legal pledge is a special protection granted to certain creditors, such as hotel owners, who can retain luggage, jewels or cash in the possession of guests, to secure payment of the expenses incurred in the establishment.

671. The subject matter is governed by Articles 1.467–1.472 of the Brazilian Civil Code. The pledge has an accessory legal nature because it requires the existence of a right of credit. In this sense, its main purpose is to fulfil the creditor's necessity to secure the loan.

§2. Configuration of the Pledge Contract under the Brazilian Civil Code

672. The Brazilian Civil Code of 2002 regulates the pledge contract in its Articles 1.431–1.472 stating that the pledge is formed when the effective possession of a movable property, susceptible to alienation, is transferred by the debtor or on his or her behalf to the creditor or his or her representative, in guarantee of the debt. In rural, industrial and commercial pledges, the object of the pledge remains in the possession of the debtor who shall safeguard and preserve it.

673. The secured creditor becomes the depositary of the object of the pledge at the moment he or she receives it.

674. Article 1.432 CC/02 refers to the publicity of the pledge. It says that the instrument of the pledge shall be registered by any party. Ordinary pledges are registered in the Registry Office of Deeds and Documents.

§3. Rights and Obligations of the Secured Creditor

675. According to Article 1.433 of the Brazilian Civil Code, the secured creditor has the right to the possession of the object of the pledge; to the retention of the object of the pledge until receipt of compensation for incurred expenses, as long as the creditor was not responsible for them; to compensation for damages arising from a defect in the object of the pledge; to the promotion of the judicial execution or the consensual sale (when authorized by contract or permitted through express mandate) of the object of the pledge; to possession of benefits rendered by the pledged asset in his or her power; and to promotion of the anticipatory sale of the object of the pledge, upon judicial authorization, whenever there is reasonable chance that the pledged asset may be lost or suffer deterioration – the amount obtained should be deposited in a bank account. The owner of the pledged asset may interrupt the sale by substituting the asset or providing a proper real guarantee. Furthermore, the creditor cannot be forced to return the pledged asset, or parts of it, until payment is met in full. A judge may, upon request by the owner, determine the sale of only one of the pledged assets or parts of it, sufficient to fulfil the debt (according to Article 1.434 CC/02).

676. Under Article 1.435 of the Brazilian Civil Code, the secured creditor has the obligation of custody of the pledged asset and the duty to compensate the owner for any loss or deterioration caused by the creditor. Moreover, he or she must adopt legal measures to keep the pledged asset safe and to inform the owner about the circumstances that imposed the adoption of such measures. He must also subtract the value of the profit obtained with the pledged asset from the incurred conservation expenses, from the applicable interest, and from the debit guaranteed. Above all the creditor must return the pledged asset, with its respective profit or accessions, once the debt is paid; and to return any pledged assets or parts of pledged assets that were not used to fulfil the payment, in the case of Article 1.433 IV CC/02.

677. Both the rights and obligations of the secured creditor might have a personal character deriving from the pledge contract; an *erga omnes* character deriving from the relationship involving rights in rem of the pledge; and a procedural law character, deriving from the possibility of selling the pledged asset upon default of payment.

§4. Rights of the Debtor

678. The debtor does not lose possession of the pledged asset, maintaining the full rights of ownership, including the right of disposition; the property of the profit and accessions of the pledged asset; the prerogative of preventing the use of the pledged asset by the creditor; the right to be compensated for any losses or deteriorations caused to the pledged asset by the creditor; the right to see the pledged assets returned once the debt is paid; and the right to the funds obtained through the judicial sale of the pledged asset, after the subtraction of the debt, applicable interest rates, and incurred expenses.

§5. Termination of the Pledge

679. Article 1.436 of the Brazilian Civil Code states that the pledge terminates when the secured obligation terminates; the pledged asset perishes; the creditor waives his or her rights; the creditor becomes the owner of the pledged asset; or the judicial adjudication, the remission or the selling of the asset is performed by the creditor or a person indicated by him or her. The resignation of the creditor is presumed when he or she consents to the private sale of the pledged asset without demanding that part of the price obtained be reserved when he or she restores the possession of the pledged asset to the debtor, or when he or she accepts the substitution of the pledged asset for another guarantee. If the creditor becomes owner merely of a part of the pledged asset, the pledge will remain in full force in regard to the other parts.

680. Requirement for the effectiveness of the pledge: under Article 1.437 of the Brazilian Civil Code, the termination of the pledge will be effective upon the cancellation of its registry, upon presentation of proper evidence. Such a disposition did not exist in the former Brazilian Civil Code of 1916.

§6. Types of Pledges

681. There are different types of pledges, depending on the assets that are objects of the pledge. There is the rural pledge (Articles 1.438–1.441 CC/02); agricultural pledge (Articles 1.442–1.443 CC/02); livestock pledge (Articles 1.444–1.450 CC/02); industrial and commercial pledge (Articles 1.447–1.450 CC/02); bond pledge (Articles 1.451–1.460 CC/02); and vehicle pledge (Articles 1.461–1.466 CC/02).

682. When an agricultural crop is offered as a pledged asset, it is considered an agricultural pledge. For obvious reasons, the pledged asset (the crop) is not transferred to the creditor; it remains in the possession of the debtor.

683. The object of the livestock pledge is livestock, i.e., animals raised for agricultural, pastoral and dairy industries.

684. An industrial pledge is related to the pledge of machines and equipment from an industrial plant. In the industrial pledge, the pledged asset remains in the possession of the debtor.

685. The commercial pledge was governed by the Brazilian Commercial Code until the 2002 Civil Code came into force. Today, with the unification of civil and commercial obligations, the Brazilian Civil Code governs the commercial pledge. This type of pledge is particularly relevant in relation to the pledge of goods stocked in warehouses (Articles 1.447–1.450 CC/02).

686. A bond pledge includes intangible assets, rights regarding movable properties that can be transferred. This type of pledge is formed through private or public instruments, registered in the Registry Office of Deeds and Documents. The original holder of the pledged right is responsible for delivering the documents that demonstrate the existence of the pledge to the creditor, unless he or she has a legitimate interest in keeping the documents in his/her possession.

687. A vehicle pledge is related to any kind of vehicle. The pledged asset should be insured against theft, damages, deterioration and damages suffered by third parties. The transfer of the ownership of the vehicle without a previous communication to the creditor anticipates the debt maturity. The duration of this type of pledge is limited to two years, with the possibility of extending that period for no longer than a further two years, through the official registration of that extension. The vehicle pledge was not present in the former Brazilian Civil Code of 1916.

Chapter 10. Loans

§1. Introduction

688. In a loan contract (*empréstimo*), one party receives a property from another party in order to use it and, later, returns it to the legitimate owner.

689. The purpose of loaning non-fungible assets is their use. The purpose of loaning fungible assets is their consumption.

690. Hence, there are two types of loans: loans for use (*comodato*) dealt with in Articles 579–585 CC/02 and loans for consumption (*mútuo*) under Articles 586–592 CC/02.

691. In this sense, the loan for use is the free lending of a non-fungible asset for the lendee's use, who is responsible for preserving the substance of the asset loaned and its return to the legitimate owner upon termination of the agreed term. For example, the loan of a beach apartment to be used during the summer of 2019.

692. The loan for use is a contract of a civil nature as it is not onerous; hence, it does not fall within the scope of consumer law. The elements of the loan for use will be addressed below.

§2. Elements of the Loan for Use

693. The first element to bear in mind is that the loan for use is a transfer of possession (for the use and fruition), free of charge and temporary, of a non-fungible asset. It differs from rental, because rental is an onerous contract. It is also different from a donation, because with donation, the transferred asset becomes the property of the donee. Loan for use is a unilateral contract, because it only generates obligations to one party, the loanee. The delivery of the good is a requirement for the contract. It is also non-onerous since it increases the assets of the loanee, without charge, while the loaner should place the good at the disposal of the loanee for his or her benefit.

694. A loan contract may be determined or undetermined. Its object can be either movable or immovable properties. Both the owner and tenant of the asset may loan it for the use of a third party. However, immovable properties require explicit authorization in writing from the owner to permit sub-letting.

695. There are also restrictions deriving from the gratuity: Article 580 of the Brazilian Civil Code prohibits guardians and curators from loaning for use assets placed under their guard, except when there is explicit authorization to do so.

696. While there is no specific requirement as to form, a loan for use should be documented if its value is greater than ten minimum wages.[188]

§3. Duties of the Parties in the Loan for Use

I. Duties of the Loanee

697. The loanee has the duty to return the asset loaned after the expiration of the contract; to use the asset in accordance with the terms of the contract and local usage. Non-observance of such duties causes the liability of the loanee, as well as termination of the agreement, according to its terms.

698. It is possible to sublet the good if this is explicitly authorized in the agreement between the parties.

699. The loanee should preserve the loaned asset as if it was his or her own property (as in rentals), according to Article 582 CC/02. He or she has to repair any damage arising from the asset's use, without any indemnification.

700. The incurred taxes are the loanee's responsibility, which does not undermine the non-onerous nature of the agreement. Extraordinary expenses should always be authorized by the loaner, so they can be compensated later. The loanee has the right of reimbursement of the expenses related to necessary improvements or renewals. If the loanee is in the possession of the asset in good faith, he or she may retain such possession until the compensation of such expenses, unless otherwise agreed (Article 584 CC/02).

701. According to Article 585 CC/02, multiple loanees are all joint debtors.

II. Duties of the Loaner or Lender

702. Loan for use becomes a bilateral agreement under the following conditions: in the case of necessary improvements or renewals, the loaner has the duty to compensate the loanee – in analogy to the dispositions that govern rental agreements. If there are damages caused by the loaned asset, the loaner has to indemnify the loanee, unless he or she was duly informed of the risks involved. If the asset perishes, the principle of *res perit domino* prevails according to Article 869 CC/02.

188. Rodrigues, Silvio. Direito Civil, dos contratos e das declarações unilaterais de vontade, vol. 3, editora Saraiva, São Paulo, 2002, p. 263.

III. Termination

703. In the case of a determined duration, the contract terminates after the time agreed. It is voidable if the loanee does not observe his or her duties. Furthermore, it may be terminated by a unilateral declaration of the loaner or the death of the loaner, if the agreement is *intuitu personae* in nature.

§4. Elements of the Loan for Consumption

I. Definition

704. Loan for consumption is the loan of a fungible asset for consumption, in which the loanee becomes the true owner of the asset loaned, having, on the one hand, the prerogative of consuming it and, on the other hand, the duty to return an equivalent asset of the same quality and value, with a generic and non-individual identification to the loaner.

705. The transfer of property is a requirement since in loans for consumption the interest in consuming the asset loaned is incompatible with its preservation. The opposite would undermine the economic purpose of the agreement.

706. Unlike loans for use, the object of the loan for consumption must be the loaner's property.

II. Characteristics

707. Loans for consumption contracts are *real* contracts that are unilateral, onerous or non-onerous and temporary and transfer property according to certain requirements.

708. They are *real* contracts because the agreement between the parties should suffice for its formation. However, according to the Brazilian Civil Code, the effective delivery of the asset is a requirement. This is a retrograde view. Without the effective delivery there is only the promise to perform a loan for consumption that can be withdrawn upon a change to the economic conditions of the loaner, leading to insolvency.

709. The contract is considered *unilateral* since only the loanee has obligations. The loaner has simply to deliver the asset.

710. Loan for consumption contracts is *non-onerous* unless otherwise agreed by the parties. However, in most cases, they are *onerous*. The unilateral feature is not incompatible with a compensation for the loan.

711. Due to the fact that returning the asset (an equivalent asset) to the owner is of essence to the contract, it is considered *temporary*.

712. Such contracts transfer the property of the asset loaned. However, the original owner does not lose his or her property rights – it is merely the means of fulfilling the contract.

713. There are subjective and objective requirements for a loan for consumption contract: subjective requirements include the capacity of the parties to assume obligations. The Roman principle *senatus consultum macedonianum,* which applies under Article 588 of the Brazilian Civil Code, states that the asset of a loan for consumption contracted with a minor, without authorization of his or her legal guardian, cannot be retrieved from the loanee or from his or her guarantors. This rule protects the inexperienced from greedy dealers. On the other hand, there is the possibility of subsequent ratification of such a contract if the person responsible for authorizing the loan for consumption subsequently authorizes it; if the minor, in the absence of such a person, had no alternative to maintain his or her regular alimentation than to contract such a loan; or if the minor has earnings arising out of his own labour. However, in the latter case, the amount charged cannot exceed the referred earnings. Another hypothesis foreseen in the Civil Code is if the loan was consumed in benefit of the minor or if the minor contracted the loan in bad faith (Article 589 CC/02).

714. Objective requirements mean that any fungible asset can be the object of loan for consumption, as long as the loaner is the true owner of such an asset – money is the most common asset in loans for consumption. The loaner normally assumes obligations; the loanee has the obligation to return an equivalent asset. The will of the parties usually determines the duration of the loan. Partial return is allowed only when agreed by the parties. In the case of mortgages or secured debts, the loanee may anticipate the full or partial return of the assets loaned to benefit from the amortization of the applicable interest rates (Decree 22.626 from 7 April 1933, Article 7 §).

715. To prove the existence of the loan for consumption, there is no applicable special requirement, such as the confession of the debt in writing or the issuance of a bond or a receipt. A loan for consumption with economic purposes is subject to interest rates under Article 591 of the Brazilian Civil Code, which will not exceed the compound interest rates referred to in Article 406 CC/02. Article 406 of the Brazilian Civil Code states that when the default interest rates have not been agreed by the parties or when they are applicable because of explicit determination of the law, the rate will be equivalent to the rate applicable to payments due to the National Treasury.[189]

---

189. *See* Arnoldo Wald, Contratos, op. cit., pp. 497 and seq.

Chapter 11. Contracts with the Government and Other Public Administrations

§1. Characteristics

716. In administrative contracts, one of the contracting parties is the public administration (*Administração Pública*), in its various facets. This type of agreement is regulated by rules previously established by the Government, in accordance with the provisions of various types of public law standards, with the purpose of preserving the collective interests.

717. The possibility of administrative contracts is based on Article 37 XXI of the Federal Constitution, regulated by the Laws n° 8.666/93, 9.032/95 and 9.648/98, 10.520/2002, as well as Decree 3.555/2000.

718. The Brazilian legislator defined the administrative contract, under Law n° 8.666/93, as follows: for the purposes of this law, any adjustment between State bodies or government entities and private individuals, where there is an agreement of wills to form bonds and stipulate reciprocal obligations, whatever denomination used, is considered a contract (Article 2).

719. The renowned scholar of administrative law, Cretella Jr. defines the administrative contract 'as a joint intention, in which the State is party, subject to the legal regime of Public Law, informed by public principles and containing "exorbitant" and "derogating" clauses of the law that is common to the parties'.[190]

720. Evidently, administrative contracts have very specific characteristics, precisely because they are contracts governed by public law standards and not by private law or customary norms. Even so, administrative contracts and private contracts have a common trait: they belong to the same family, i.e., they are consents to be bound to a clearly specific aim, so far as permitted by law. There are various examples of public contracts, among the most common are those for collaboration, supply, service, assignment, award of public work, and the most widely used, for obvious reasons, the concession contract.

721. An interesting point regarding contracts with public administration concerns the interpretation of the clauses based on the rules of public law, which favour the administrative body, rather than private law. Nevertheless, despite the fact that administrative contracts should always be guided by public law, in a supplemental role private law rules may also apply to the administrative contract.

722. To illustrate this point regarding the hermeneutics of administrative contracts, we refer to Article 54 of the Bidding Law (*Lei de Licitações e Contratos*, Law

190. V. José Cretela Jr. Curso de Direito Administrativo, Editora Forense, Rio de Janeiro, 1997, p. 331.

n° 8.666 from 21 June 1993): *Administrative contracts ruled by this law are governed by the terms and principles of the Public Law; additionally, the principles of the general theory of contracts and the provisions of Private Law apply.*

723. It shows the close connection between public and private law, in the case of contracts. In relation to administrative jurisdiction, unlike other Latin American countries which are greatly inspired by French law, such as Colombia, Brazil has no administrative courts. Conflicts involving this issue are decided before civil courts.

724. In the private domain, freedom of contract has, in accordance with the Civil Code, some limits, such as the respect for Public Order and Good Morals, and the respect for the social function of the contract (Article 421 CC/02).

725. Aside from these limitations, which are considered mandatory, the parties in the field of private law contracts are almost completely free with regard to the design of their contracts, which is not the case with regard to government contracts because the money is public. This is because in the sphere of public law, there is greater rigidity in the procedural and substantive requirements arising from the law to which the administration is subject. On the other hand, the law also gives the public administration the power and privilege to regulate, modify and solve such contracts.

726. Administrative contracts have very peculiar characteristics and in order to better explain them, we present below the standards required by law for the validity of such contracts.

727. Capacity: Capacity is an essential element for a party in a contract. In an administrative contract, the private party must meet requirements stipulated by the administration. In this respect, capacity has the connotation of *legal qualification*, that is, the candidate contractor must submit to the requirements described in the law of tender in order to participate in the selection or in the contracting.

728. Formalism: While in private contracts a certain formalism may be a prerequisite for the validity of the agreement (according to Articles 104, 185 and 166 III CC/02), formalism may occasionally be required for security purposes. However, in government contracts, failure to fulfil a formality that should have been observed will not invalidate the contract. The law imposes external and internal requirements for the preparation of contracts with the administration, such as the prohibition of verbal agreements except those involving small purchases with prompt payment, regarded as those involving values not exceeding 5% of the limit laid down in Article 23 II ‘a’ of Law n° 8.666/90. According to Article 60 of the Law n° 8.666/90, contracts and their amendments will be issued in the offices concerned, which should maintain chronological records of the contract signatories and of all the relevant documents and systematic records. Verbal contracts with the administration are null and have no effect.

729. Moreover, according to Article 61 of the Law n° 8.666/90, every contract shall state the names of the parties and their representatives, the purpose, the act that authorized its drafting, the bidding process number, or waiver of unenforceability, subjecting contractors to the rules of this law and the contractual terms.

730. Bilateralism: The contract with the administration must necessarily be bilateral. It should contain a correlation of rights and obligations for both parties, unlike in private law, where some contracts are not bilateral, for example, donation and loan for use contracts.

731. Commutability: Commutability between the benefits of the parties involved in the administrative contract is required. There must be equivalence between the benefits of the parties involved in the contract.

732. Object: In private law, the object of the contract shall be licit and possible. These same requirements are demanded in relation to the purpose of an administrative agreement.

733. The administrative contract is onerous, providing payment for the provision of the counterparty.

734. An important element of the administrative contract is mutual trust. When contracting, the public administration takes into account the predicates and conditions of the contract, conditions that are required in the bidding process. Hence the administrative contract is considered *intuitu personae*.

735. The administrative contract imposes an administrative law regime, because the contract, in addition to a public purpose, must also have the purpose of administrative law.

736. Exorbitant clauses (*cláusulas exorbitantes*): The expressed or implied existence of exorbitant or supremacy clauses, indicating the superiority of the public administration in relation to the private entity, is one of the most peculiar aspects of administrative contracts, especially when compared to contracts in private law. There are numerous situations where such clauses are present, further differentiating the administrative contract from private law. In the words of Edmir Netto de Araújo[191] *the Administration when contracting, does not give up its 'puissance publique', but instead guides the contract, supervising the acts of the particular contractor, applying penalties, giving benefits, determining procedures, finally, by imposing subjection based on the public interest.*

737. Moreover, regarding this particular aspect of administrative contract, it is important to refer to the legal rules governing such exorbitant clauses. According to Article 58 of the aforementioned Bidding Law, such clauses, although not mentioned in the contract, affect the agreement. As an example, there is a clause that

191. Op. ment. p. 724.

allows the state, supported by the claim to represent the public interest, to unilaterally change certain contractual conditions. This power of the administration to unilaterally modify the contract is called mutability (*mutabilidade*). The administration's most severe unilateral contractual modification is withdrawal. The doctrine defines mutability as *the State power-duty to change one or more of its contractual clauses due to the public interest.*

§2. Types of Administrative Contracts

738. In Brazilian law, there are two types of administrative contracts: on the one hand, private contracts of the public administration are, regardless of their administrative nature, ruled by private law. In this case, the administration behaves like a private entity, and does not receive benefits or privileges of any kind. In this type of contract, only the contractor's capacity based on the administrative rules is taken into account. Examples of such contracts are loans, when the administration is a lessee of private property, or when the administration pursues an insurance or financing contract, etc.

739. The second type of administrative contract, which is considered essentially administrative, is ruled by public law. The peculiarities listed above are present in this type of contract – especially the power to modify the contract and the inclusion of exorbitant clauses, as mentioned above.

740. Furthermore, pursuant to Article 37 XXI of the Federal Constitution and Article 57 § 1 of the Bidding Law, the government should maintain the economic balance of its contracts, in order to guarantee the original terms of the agreement. The proper compliance of the guarantee of economic and financial balance of the contract is foreseen in the Federal Constitution, which states that the law may not affect the vested right, the perfect juridical act and the res judicata (Article 5 XXXVI CF). Economic and financial balance is considered a vested right in the contract.

741. On the other hand, the administration may, based on rule of public policy, unilaterally modify the contract, with no prior waiver of that right being permitted (Article 65 I of the Bidding Law, Law n° 8.666/93). Moreover, on the basis of public interest, the administration is authorized by law to unilaterally withdraw from the contract, which must be justified and in writing. The causes that permit the modification, revision or termination may be based on different theories, such as 'the fact of the Prince', 'the fact of the public administration', of the Alteration of Circumstances and Force Majeure, which reflect the clause *rebus sic stantibus*.

742. All the above-mentioned theories apply to private law contracts. However, there is an idiosyncrasy in the administrative contract without a counterpart in private contracts; that is a party that suffers damage due to the public power cannot allege 'exception due to unfulfilled contract', as recognized in Article 476 of the

Civil Code (*exceptio non adimpleti contractus*), according to which one party is not obliged to fulfil their obligation if the other party fails to fulfil their obligations under the contract.

743. The private party is not authorized to invoke that power because of the principle of the continuity of public service, unless there is a legal provision for this purpose (Article 78 of the Bidding Law, Law n° 8.666/93). Another aspect that highlights the public part of the contract is the requirement of a guarantee offer (deposit in cash, general government debt securities or suretyship) for the contractor to comply with the contract, which is chosen from the options provided for in the law. Once the contract is performed, the warranty is returned, as stated in Article 56 §1 of the Bidding Law.

744. Guarantees are accepted *in natura*, as insurances or as bank guarantees.

745. The most commonly prescribed administrative contracts are the following: public works contracts, service, supply, provision of public service and public works, etc.

746. To conclude this brief study on administrative contracts in Brazil, it is important to stress that many disputes arise from this kind of contract, as a result of their complexity, the variety of rules on the matter and, above all, the lack of a specialized court in its demarcation. Thus, since 1996, Brazil has been equipped with an arbitration law, which is expected to peacefully solve conflicts involving administrative contracts.

747. It is worth mentioning that for more than a century, lawyers, such as Rui Barbosa and Mendes Pimentel, analysed the competence of the Brazilian Public Administration to sign arbitration clauses, as the scholar Selma Lemes said in her important work Arbitragem na Administração Pública, Fundamentos Jurídicos e Eficiência Econômica.[192]

748. Recently, the new Law of Arbitration (*Lei de Arbitragem*, Law n° 13.129 from 26 May 2015, entered into force on 27 July 2015) has authorized the public administration to take part in arbitration. However, the administration may not choose the fairness (equity) as the rule of the arbitration. Moreover, the principle of public interest, which is important in the administrative sphere, must be observed.[193]

192. Editora Quartier Latin, Rio de Janeiro, 2007, p. 273.

193. *See* Commentary about this new Law, 'La récente modernisation du système législative brésilien', in Revue Internationale de Droit Comparé, éditeur Société de Législation Comparée, Paris, July/September 2015, n°3, pp. 843 et seq.

Chapter 12. Partnership Agreements

749. According to Article 981 CC/02, partnership agreements (articles of association, *contrato de sociedade*) are celebrated by people who mutually undertake to contribute with goods or services to the exercise of an economic activity and to share the results with each other. According to the sole paragraph of the same article, the activity may be limited to the achievement of one or more determined business purposes.

750. The partnership is formed by a multilateral agreement, with the partners undertaking mutual obligations.

751. For the exercise of a partnership's activities, it is necessary to adopt a business name. This 'denomination' must be adopted in accordance with the provisions of Book II of the Special Part of the Civil Code, Title IV, Chapter II, Article 1.155 and its sole paragraph. The denomination of partnerships, associations and foundations equates to the corporate name for the sake of legal protection.

752. It should be noted that the business name has legal protection, including protection under the Law of Industrial Property (*Lei de propriedade industrial*).

753. The doctrine points to the coexistence of a right and a duty to the business name. On the one hand, the right to a business name comes from the fact that legal entities have the right to an identity. On the other, the duty to have a business name complies with the rules of public order, which require businesses to have an identification, so that they are identifiable by the society and by the State.

754. Moreover, it is important to distinguish between the business name and the brand. The business name is the distinctive title of the entrepreneur or partnership, which provides a legal personality while being subject to the law. By contrast, the brand identifies the product offered by the entrepreneur or partnership.

755. According to Law nº 8.934/1994 from 18 November 1994, which governs the Public Registry of Companies and Similar Activities, the business name is subject to the principles of truthfulness (authenticity or reality), novelty and exclusivity (Article 34).

756. The business name is presented in two ways: on the one hand, the 'name' (distinctive title of the entrepreneur or partnership); and, on the other, the 'denomination', which identifies the business, distinguishing it from the others. Put simply, the characteristic feature of the business name is the name itself, while the characteristic feature of the denomination is the business' objective.[194]

194. Justino Vasconcelos, Firmas, editora Forense, Rio de Janeiro, 1957, nº 14, p. 31.

757. The partnership must have a purpose: most companies operate in order to achieve results of a financial nature, although they may possibly have no financial goal. Furthermore, the partnership's activity must be lawful and possible.

758. It is important to highlight that a partnership is constituted through a partnership agreement (articles of association), acquiring legal personality with the entry in the appropriate registry and according to the law, to the articles of association, and to the terms of Article 985 CC/02.

759. While the partnership is not yet registered, it is considered a de facto partnership or irregular partnership, or, according to the Civil Code, an 'ordinary partnership' (*sociedade em comum*, Article 986 CC/02).

760. A partnership agreement (articles of association) is formed by consensus; it is obviously onerous and commutative, since the partners are aware of the value and content of their respective duties and benefits.

761. As to its bilateral or multilateral nature, its classification in this respect depends on the number of partners, if there are two partners (bilateral) or more than two (multilateral). Interestingly, the law provides that, depending on the type of legal entity, there are a minimum number of members.

762. Partnerships are regulated by the articles of association, and the partners must bow to their terms, and abide by them faithfully, as in this sphere the fundamental principle of the contract, the *pacta sunt servanda,* prevails. Another very important element in partnership agreements is the *affectio societatis*, an element that brings together the efforts of partners, in view of the common objectives and purposes of the partnership.

763. The partners must contribute to the assets of the partnership, forming what is called the 'partnership's assets' (*capital social*) – a contribution which may be in cash or other assets, provided they are economically assessable (movable assets, immovable properties, tangible or intangible). It is clear that the partners share the profits and also bear the losses of the partnership (Article 1.007 CC/02).

764. If there are any gaps in the articles of association or any conflicts between the terms of the articles of association and the law, the law shall apply.

765. Brazilian law regulated this issue in the Commercial Code of 1850, which remained in force until 2003, when the 2002 Civil Code entered into force, unifying civil and commercial obligations. From that date on, commercial law took the denomination of corporate law (*Direito Empresarial*). One interesting aspect regarding this issue concerns the influence of the Brazilian Law of Corporations, Law nº 6.404/1976, on the current corporate law, constituting a truly independent system in this field, while remaining as a sparse piece of legislation.

766. One important theme concerns the termination of the partnership due to the death of a partner. According to Article 1.028 CC/02, unless the agreement provides otherwise, the deceased partner's shares shall be liquidated, if the remaining partners choose to dissolve the partnership. The partners may also arrange for the replacement of the deceased partner by agreement with the heirs.

767. With regard to the termination of the partnership, Article 1.033 CC/02 provides that it shall be dissolved at the end of its term, unless after the end of the term and without the opposition of any partners the partnership does not enter into liquidation, in which case its term shall extend indefinitely. Moreover, it may be dissolved: by the unanimous consent of the partners; by a resolution supported by an absolute majority of the shareholders, in partnerships with an indefinite term; and with the extinction of the authorization to conduct business, according to the law. Additionally, the partnership ends in the case of a lack of plurality of partners, which is not reconstituted within the term of 180 days. However, this provision does not apply if the remaining partner applies to re-register the public limited company as an individual limited liability company in the Public Registry of Companies.

768. Also, a partnership may be judicially dissolved upon request by any of the partners, when its association is cancelled, or when the partnership's purpose is exhausted, or the impossibility to execute the partnership's purpose is verified (Article 1.034 CC/02).

769. Pursuant to Article 1.035 CC/02, the partnership agreement (articles of association) may provide for other causes of termination to be verified in court, if challenged.

770. The appropriate government instances are currently considering a bill to reinstitute a new Commercial Code, independent from the Civil Code, to meet the demands of those dedicated to commercial activity. This bill does not have the unanimous approval of Brazilian legal scholars. However, one of its motivations is well founded, that is, a new Commercial Code should inhibit the application of the Consumer Protection Code in transactions between business entities, which is a practice widely found in Brazilian case law and also supported by legal experts.[195]

195. For this matter *see* Arnoldo Wald, Comentários ao Novo Código Civil, Livro II, do Direito de Empresa, Arts 966–1.195, vol. XIV, coord. Sálvio de Figueiredo Teixeira, Editora Forense, Rio de Janeiro, 2005.

Selected Bibliography

Amico, Manuel García. *Condiciones generales de los contratos.* Madrid: Editorial Tecnos, 1965.

Araújo Netto, Edmir. *Curso de direito administrativo.* 6. ed. São Paulo: Saraiva, 2014.

Assis, Araken de. *Contratos nominados.* São Paulo: Revista dos Tribunais, 2005.

Azevedo, Álvaro Villaça de. *Teoria geral dos contratos típicos e atípicos.* 3. ed. São Paulo: Atlas, 2009.

Azevedo, Antonio Junqueira de. A boa fé na formação dos contratos. *Revista Direito do Consumidor,* São Paulo, n. 3, p. 83, 1992.

Azevedo, Antonio Junqueira de. Princípios do novo direito contratual e desregulamentação do mercado. *Revista dos Tribunais*, São Paulo, n. 750, pp. 113–120, abr. 1998.

Becker, Anelise. As garantias implícitas no direito brasileiro e em perspectiva comparativista. *Revista Direito do Consumidor*, São Paulo, n. 09, pp. 69–91, jan/mar. 1994.

Beraldo, Leonardo de Faria. *Curso de arbitragem.* São Paulo: Atlas, 2014.

Beviláqua, Clóvis. *Código Civil comentado.* Rio de Janeiro: Livraria Francisco Alves, 1959, v. 1.

Bonnet, David. *Cause et condition dans les actes juridiques.* Paris: LGDJ, 2005.

Brandelli, Leonardo. Abstração e causalidade entre o plano real e o obrigacional e as espécies registrais imobiliárias. *Revista de Direito Imobiliário*, São Paulo, v. 79, ano 38, pp. 85–124, jul./.dez. 2015.

Brandelli, Leonardo. *Teoria geral do direito notarial.* 2. ed. São Paulo: Saraiva, São Paulo, 2007.

Bussani, Mauro. *I contratti nuovi.* Milano: Giuffrè Editore, 1989.

Carbonnier, Jean. *Le flexible droit.* Paris: LGDJ, 1963.

Cardoso, Patrícia. Oponibilidade dos efeitos dos contratos determinandos da responsabilidade civil de terceiro, que coopera com o devedor na violação do pacto contratual. *Revista Trimestral de Direito Civil,* Rio de Janeiro, v. 20, p. 130, out/dez. 2004.

Caruso, Daniela. *Culpa in contrahendo:* l'esperienza statunitense e quella italiana a confronto. Milano: Giuffrè Editore, 1993.

Cavalieri Filho, Sérgio. *Programa de Direito do consumidor*. Rio de Janeiro: Atlas, 2019.

Selected Bibliography

Chaloub, Melhim Namem. *Trust, perspectivas do direito contemporâneo na transmissão da propriedade para administração de investimentos e garantia.* Rio de Janeiro: Renovar, 2001.

Costa Neves, Arnaldo Gabriel. *Dos contratos de contrapartidas no comércio internacional.* Coimbra: Almedina, 2003.

Costa, Mário Júlio de Almeida *Direito das obrigações.* 6. ed. Coimbra: Almedina, 1994.

Couto e Silva, Clóvis do. A teoria da causa no direito privado. In: Fradera, Véra Jacob de (Org). *O direito privado brasileiro na visão de Clóvis do Couto e Silva.* 2. ed. rev. Porto Alegre: Livraria do Advogado, 2014, p. 57.

Couto e Silva, Clóvis do. *A teoria da base do negócio jurídico.* In: Fradera, Véra Jacob de (Org). *O direito privado brasileiro na visão de Clóvis do Couto e Silva.* 2. ed. rev. Porto Alegre: Livraria do Advogado, 2014, p. 87.

Couto e Silva, Clóvis do. Direito material e processual em matéria de prova. *Revista de Processo,* São Paulo, v.13, jan. 1979, pp. 135–146.

Couto e Silva, Clóvis do. *A obrigação como processo.* São Paulo: José Bushastki, 1976.

Cretela Junior, José. *Curso de direito administrativo.* Rio de Janeiro: Forense, 1997.

David, René. 'L'Imprévision dans les Droits européens'. *Études offertes à Alfred Jauffret.* Faculté de Droit et de Sciences politiques d' Aix-Marseille, 1974, pp. 211–229.

David, René. Le rôle de la pensée juridique française dans la formation et évolution des droits étrangers. *Revue de l'enseignement supérieur.* n. 2, pp. 97–100, 1960.

David, René. Structure et idéologie du droit brésilien. *Cahiers de Législation et de Bibliographie Juridique de l'Amérique Latine,* n. 17/18, pp. 7–20, jan./jui. 1954.

Dawson, John. The general clauses viewed from a distance, *RabelsZ,* 1977, jg. 41, pp. 441–456, Heft 03.

Delgado, Mário Luiz; Alves, Jones Figueiredo (Orgs.). *Novo Código Civil:* questões controvertidas. São Paulo: Método, 2004, v. 2.

Ennecerus, Ludwig; Kipp, Theodor; Wolff, Martin. *Tratado de derecho civil.* Barcelona: Bosch, 1953, t. 2.

Espinola, Eduardo. *Manual do Código Civil brasileiro*: dos factos jurídicos. Rio de Janeiro: Editora J. Ribeiro Santos, 1926, v. 3, parte 2.

Fabre-Magnan, Muriel. *De l'obligation d'information dans les contrats.* Paris: LGDJ, 1992.

Faoro, Raymundo. *Os donos do poder.* Porto Alegre: Globo, 1973.

Farnworth, E. Allan. Good faith in contract performance. In: Beatson, Jack; Friedman, Daniel (Dir.) *Good faith and fault in contract law.* Oxford: Clarendon Press, 1997, pp. 153–190.

Feiten Wingert Ody, Lisiane. *Einführung in das brasilianische Recht.* München: C.H. Beck, 2016.

Feiten Wingert Ody. *Direito e Arte*: O direito da arte brasileiro sistematizado a partir do paradigm alemão. São Paulo: Marcial Pons, 2018.

Feiten Wingert Ody. O conceito de consumidor e noção de vulnerabilidade nos países do Mercosul. In: Revista de direito do consumidor, v. 16, n. 64, pp. 80–108, out./dez. 2007.

Feiten Wingert Ody. Der allgemeine Teil des brasilianischen Zivilgesetzbuchs: geschichtlicher Hintergrund und systematische Überlegungen. In: Feiten Wingert Ody, Lisiane; Menke, Fabiano; Waadt, Steffen (Hrsg.). *Studien zum deutsch-brasilianischen Recht:* ein Beitrag zum Deutschland-Brasilien Jahr 2013, München, Grin, 2013.

Ferrari, Franco. Abstraktionsprinzip, Traditionsprinzip e consensualismo nel trasferimento di beni mobili: una superabile divaricazione? *Rivista de Diritto Civile,* Milano, n.6, pp. 729–757, 1993.

Fonseca, Rodrigo Garcia da. Considerações sobre o *trust* (fidúcia) no direito comparado. *Revista Forense,* Rio de Janeiro, vol. 334, pp. 153–190, abr./jun. 1996.

Forgioni, Paula *Contrato de distribuição.* 3. ed. São Paulo: Revista dos Tribunais, 2014.

Fradera, Véra Jacob de. Dano pré-contratual, uma análise comparativa a partir de três sistemas jurídicos: o continental europeu, o latino americano e o americano do norte. *Revista de Informação Legislativa,* v. 34, n. 136, pp. 169–179, out./dez. 1997.

Fradera, Véra Jacob de. O valor do silêncio no código civil brasileiro. In: Alvim, Arruda; César, Joaquim Portes de Cerqueira; Rosas, Roberto. *Aspectos controvertidos do novo Código Civil:* estudos em homenagem ao ministro José Carlos Moreira Alves. São Paulo: Revista dos Tribunais, 2003, pp. 569–582.

Fradera, Véra Jacob de. Informar ou não informar, eis a questão! In: Fradera, Véra Jacob de; Martins-Costa, Judith (Orgs.). *Estudos de direito privado e processual civil em homenagem a Clóvis do Couto e Silva.* São Paulo: Revista dos Tribunais, 2014, pp. 231–253.

Fradera, Véra Jacob de. La culture juridique et l'acculturation du droit rapport national bresilien. In: Cordero, Jorge A. Sánchez (Ed.). *Legal Culture And Legal Transplants:* Reports To The XVIIIth International Congress of Comparative Law, Washington, D.C., v. 1, p. 195, 2010.

Fradera, Véra Jacob de. La récente modernisation du système législatif brésilien. In: *Revue Internationale de Droit Comparé,* n. 3, Paris, pp. 847–852, juil./sep. 2015.

Fraga, Francisco Jordano. *La responsabilidad contractual.* Madrid: Editorial Civitas, 1987.

Gauvard, Claude; Libera, Alain de; Ziruk, Michel (Dir.). *Dictionnaire du moyen âge.* Paris: Presses Universitaires de France-PUF, 2002.

Gazalle, Gustavo Kratz. *O conceito de mora no código civil de 2002.* Porto Alegre: Sérgio Antonio Fabris Editor, 2008.

Ghestin, Jacques. *L'utile et le juste dans les contrats.* Paris: Sirey, 1981.

Guarnieri, Attilio. *La circulation des modèles au cours des deux derniers siècles.* In: Rapports nationaux italiens au XIIIè, Congrès International de Droit Comparé, Milano, Giuffrè, 1990.

Gomes, Orlando. *Introdução ao direito civil.* Rio de Janeiro: Forense, 1974.

Gomes, Orlando. *Contratos.* Atual. por Humberto Theodoro Junior. Rio de Janeiro: Forense, 2003.

Gonçalves, Carlos Roberto. *Direito civil brasileiro.* 3. ed. São Paulo: Saraiva, 2007, v. 3.

Grau, Eros Roberto. *A ordem econômica na constituição de 1988:* interpretação e crítica. São Paulo: Revista dos Tribunais, 2002.

Guilherme, Luiz Fernando do Vale de Almeida. *Manual de arbitragem.* 2. ed. São Paulo: Método, 2007.

Haical, Gustavo. *Contrato de agência.* São Paulo: Revista dos Tribunais, 2012.

Jhering, Rudolf von. De la culpa in contrahendo. Des dommages: intérêts dans les conventions nulles ou restées imparfaites. In: *Oeuvres Choisis,* Paris: Marescq, 1903, Trad. O. De Meulenaere, t. 2, pp .03–100.

Josserand, Louis. *Essais de téléologie juridique: De l'esprit des droits et de leur relativité: théorie dite de l'abus des droits*, reed., Paris: Dalloz, 2006.

Kfouri Neto, Miguel. *Responsabilidade civil do médico.* 8. ed. São Paulo: Revista dos Tribunais, 2013.

Konder, Carlos Nelson. Erro, dolo e coação: autonomia e confiança na celebração dos negócios jurídicos. In: Teixeira, Ana Carolina Brochado; Ribeiro, Gustavo Pereira Leite (Orgs.). *Manual de teoria geral do direito civil.* Belo Horizonte: Del Rey, 2011, pp. 609–631.

Larenz, Karl. *Derecho civil.* Parte general. Madrid: Editoriales de Derecho Reunidas, 1978.

Larenz, Karl. *Geschäftsgrundlage und Vertragserfüllung.* Berlin: C.H. Beck, 1957.

Latina, Mathias. *Essai sur la condition.* Paris: LGDJ, 2009.

Lemes, Selma. *Arbitragem na administração pública.* São Paulo: Quartier Latin, 2007.

Leonardo, Rodrigo Xavier. A prescrição no código civil brasileiro (ou o jogo dos sete erros). *Revista da Faculdade de Direito da Universidade Federal do Paraná,* v. 51, pp. 101–120, 2010.

Leonardo, Rodrigo Xavier.. A função social dos contratos: ponderações após o primeiro biênio de vigência do Código Civil. In: Canezin, Claudete Carvalho. *Arte jurídica:* biblioteca científica de direito civil e processo civil da Universidade Estadual de Londrina. Curitiba: Juruá, 2005, v. 2.

Leal, Victor Nunes. Classificação das normas jurídicas. *Revista de direito administrativo,* São Paulo, n. 2, v. 2, 1945, pp. 931–948.

Lima, Alvino. A interferência de terceiros na violação do contrato. *Revista dos Tribunais,* São Paulo, n. 315, v. 51, n. 315, pp. 14–30, jan. 1962.

Limbach, Francis. *Le consentement contractuel à l'épreuve des conditions générales:* de l'utilité du concept de déclaration de volonté, Paris: LGDJ, 2004.

Liquidatto, Alexandre. *O contrato de penhor.* 2012. Tese (Doutorado em Direito) – Programa de Pós-graduação em Direito, Universidade de São Paulo – USP, São Paulo, 2012.

Lôbo, Paulo Luiz Netto. *Comentários ao Código Civil.* Parte especial. Arts. 481 a 564. São Paulo: Saraiva, 2003, v. 6.

Lopez, Tereza Ancona. *Comentários ao Código Civil.* Parte especial. Arts 565 a 652. São Paulo: Saraiva, 2003, v. 7.

Ludwig, Marcos de Campos. *Usos e costumes no processo obrigacional.* São Paulo: Revista dos Tribunais, 2005.

Macedo JR., Ronaldo Porto. *Contratos relacionais e defesa do consumidor.* São Paulo: Max Limonad, 1998.

Maluf, Carlos Alberto Dabus. *As condições no direito civil.* 3. ed. São Paulo: Saraiva, 2011.

Marques, Claudia; Bessa, Leonardo; Herman V. Benjamin, Antonio. *Manual de Direito do Consumidor*. São Paulo: RT, 2017.

Martins-Costa, Judith. *Comentários ao novo código civil.* 2. ed. Rio de Janeiro: Forense, v. 5, t. 1.

Martins-Costa, Judith. Um aspecto da obrigação de indenizar: notas para uma sistematização dos deveres pré-negociais de proteção no direito civil brasileiro. In: Mendes, Gilmar Ferreira; Campos, Diogo Leite de; Martins, Ives Gandra (Coords.). *A evolução do direito no século XXI.* Estudos em homenagem ao professor Arnoldo Wald. Coimbra: Almedina, 1ª ed. Coimbra: Almedina, 2007, pp. 301–355.

Martins-Costa, Judith. Os negócios fiduciários: considerações sobre a possibilidade de acolhimento do *trust* no direito brasileiro. *Revista dos Tribunais*, São Paulo, v. 657, pp. 37–50, 1990.

Martins-Costa, Judith. A boa-fé e o seguro no novo código civil brasileiro: virtualidades da boa-fé como regra e como cláusula geral. In: *III Fórum de direito do seguro,* São Paulo: Manuais Técnicos de Seguros, 2003.

Martins, Sérgio Pinto *Instituições de direito público e privado.* 8 ed. São Paulo: Atlas, 2008, t. 19.

Marty, Gabriel & Raynaud, Pierre *Droit civil:* introduction générale à l'étude du droit. 2 ed., Paris: Sirey, 1972.

Mello, Marcos Bernardes de. *Teoria do fato jurídico:* plano da existência. 13. ed. São Paulo: Saraiva, 2014.

Mello, Marcos Bernardes de. *Teoria do fato jurídico:* plano da validade. 7. ed. São Paulo: Saraiva, 2006.

Mello, Marcos Bernardes de. *Teoria do fato jurídico:* plano da eficácia. 1ª parte. 3. ed. São Paulo: Saraiva, 2007.

Menezes Cordeiro, Manuel da Rocha, *Direito das obrigações.* Lisboa: Associação Acadêmica da Faculdade de Direito de Lisboa, 1980.

Michelon, Cláudio Fortunato Junior. *Direito restitutório:* enriquecimento sem causa, pagamento indevido, gestão de negócios. São Paulo: Revista dos Tribunais, 2007.

Moreira Alves, José Carlos. *A parte geral do Projeto de Código Civil Brasileiro*: subsídios históricos para o novo Código Civil Brasileiro. São Paulo: Saraiva, 2003.

Moreira, Carlos Roberto Barbosa. Conversão do negócio jurídico. In Teixeira, Ana Carolina Brochado; Ribeiro, Gustavo Pereira Leite (Orgs.). *Manual de teoria geral do direito civil.* Belo Horizonte: Del Rey, 2011, pp. 677–691.

Mota Pinto, Carlos Alberto da. *Teoria geral do direito civil.* Coimbra: Coimbra Editora, 1985.

Nanni, Giovanni Ettore. *Direito civil e arbitragem.* São Paulo: Atlas, 2014.

Oertel, Roberta. *Le contrat international de distribution:* concession et franchise. Comparaison France-Brésil. Paris: Bruylant, 2016.

Palandt, Otto. *Bürgerliches Gesetzbuch.* 52 Aufl., München: C. H. Beck, 1988.

Palmer, Vernon V. The style of legislation in the United States: narrative norms and constraining norms, *The American Journal of Comparative Law,* Georgetown University Center, v. 42, pp. 15–22, 1994.

Pedamon, Michel. *Le droit allemand.* Paris: Press Universitaires de France – PUF, 1985.

Pereira, Caio Mário da Silva. *Instituições de direito civil.* Atual. por Régis Fichtner. Rio de Janeiro: Forense, 2003, v. 3.

Pinto Monteiro, Antonio. *Cláusula penal e indemnização.* Coimbra: Almedina, 1990.

Pontes De Miranda, Francisco Cavalcanti. *Tratado de direito privado.* 3. ed. São Paulo: Revista dos Tribunais, 1984, t. 44.

Pontes De Miranda, Francisco Cavalcanti. *Tratado de direito privado.* 3. ed. Rio de Janeiro: Borsoi, 1972, t. 60.

Popp, Carlyle. *Responsabilidade civil pré-negocial.* Curitiba: Juruá, 2001.

Rabello, Alfredo Mordachai. The style of legislation: narrative norms and constraining norms, *Isreali Reports to the XIV International Congress of Comparative Law*, Jerusalem, Harry and Michael Sacher Institute for Legislative Research and Comparative Law, 1994.

Reale, Miguel *Estudos preliminares do código civil.* São Paulo: Revista dos Tribunais, 2003.

Requião, Rubens. O contrato de concessão de venda com exclusividade (concessão comercial), *Revista da Faculdade de Direito UFPR*, 1972, pp. 207–246

Rodrigues, Sílvio. *Direito civil:* direito das coisas. 28. ed. São Paulo: Saraiva, 2007, v. 05.

Rosenvald, Nelson. Da interpretação do negócio jurídico. In: Lotufo, Renan; Nanni, Giovanni Ettore (Orgs.). *Teoria geral do direito civil.* São Paulo: Atlas, 2008, pp. 409–431.

Sacco, Rodolfo. Le transfert de la proprieté des choses mobilières déterminées par acte entre vifs en droit comparé. *Rivista di Diritto Civile,* Milano, n. 4, p. 442, gen./feb. 1979.

Salas, Acdeel. De la exceptio non adimpleti contractus. *Revista del Derecho Comercial e de las Obligaciones,* Buenos Aires, t. 1, p. 655, 2012.

Sampaio, Rodolfo Barreto Junior. Estado de perigo e lesão. In Teixeira, Ana Carolina Brochado; Ribeiro, Gustavo Pereira Leite (Orgs.). *Manual de teoria geral do direito civil.* Belo Horizonte: Del Rey, 2011, pp. 633–639.

Santos, Gildo dos. A fiança. In: Franciulli Netto, Domingos; Mendes, Gilmar Ferreira; Martins, Ives Gandra (Orgs.) *O novo código civil.* Estudos em homenagem ao prof. Miguel Reale. São Paulo: LTr, 2003.

Schipani, Sandro. Il codice civile spagnolo come ponte fra sistema latinoamericano e codice europei. *Rivista de Diritto Civile*, c v. 40, n. 2, pp. 359–397, t. 1, mar./apr., 1994.

Schmidt, Jan. Zivilrechtskodifikation in Brasilien. Tübingen: Mohr Siebeck, 2009.

Schmidt, Joana. International encyclopaedia of law of contracts. In: Herbots, Jacques (Volume Editor); Blanpain, Roger (General Editor); Hendrickx, Frank (General Editor). *Kluwer law international,* The Netherlands, 1999.

Silva, Jorge Cesa Ferreira da. Adimplemento e extinção das obrigações. In: Reale Junior, Miguel; Martins-Costa, Judith (Orgs.). *Estudos em homenagem ao professor Miguel Reale.* São Paulo: Revista dos Tribunais, 2007.

Steiner, Renata C. *Descumprimento contratual, boa fé e violação positiva do contrato.* São Paulo: Quartier Latin, 2014.

Tallon, Denis. Pourquoi parler de faute contractuelle? In: *Études en l'honneur de Gerard Cornu.* Paris: Press Universitaires de France – PUF, 1994, p. 429.

Tartuce, Flávio. *Manual de direito civil.* São Paulo: Método, 2012.

Theodoro Junior, Humberto. Da prescrição e decadência no novo código civil brasileiro. In: Arruda Alvim Neto, José Manoel de; Cesar, Joaquim Portes de Cerqueira; Rosas, Roberto (Orgs.). *Aspectos controvertidos do novo código civil.* Estudos em homenagem ao ministro José Carlos Moreira Alves. São Paulo: Revista dos Tribunais, 2003, pp. 315–324.

Tutikian, Priscila Sansone. *O silêncio na formação dos contratos.* Porto Alegre: Livraria do Advogado, 2009.

Vasconcelos, Justino. *Firmas.* Rio de Janeiro: Forense, 1957.

Vasconcelos, Pedro Pais de: *Contratos atípicos.* Coimbra: Almedina, 1995.

Venosa, Silvio de Salvo. *Código civil interpretado.* 2. ed. São Paulo: Atlas, 2011.

Venosa, Silvio de Salvo. *Direito civil*: contratos em espécie. 9. ed. São Paulo: Atlas, 2009, volume 03.

Venosa, Silvio de Salvo. *Direito civil:* direito reais. 7. ed. São Paulo: Atlas, 2007, v. 05.

Venosa, Silvio de Salvo. *Lei do inquilinato comentada*: doutrina e prática. Lei n. 8.245, de 18-10-1991. 7. ed. São Paulo: Atlas, 2004.

Vieira, Iacyr de Aguilar. Compra e venda e a transferência da propriedade. Modelos causaise abstratos. *Revista dos Tribunais*, São Paulo, v. 88, n.765, pp. 59–77, jul. 1999.

Viney, Geneviève. L'inéxecution du contrat: pour une autre présentation. *Revue Trimestrielle de Droit Civil,* v. 93, n. 2, pp. 223–238, avr./juin. 1994.

Viney, Geneviève.. La responsabilité contractuelle en question. In: *Le contrat au début du XXè. siècle:* Études ofertes à Jacques Ghestin. Paris: LGDJ, 2001, p. 921.

Wald, Arnoldo (Org.). *Doutrinas Essenciais:* arbitragem e mediação. São Paulo: Revista dos Tribunais, São Paulo, 2014, v. 1–7.

Wald, Arnoldo (Org.).. *Comentários ao novo código civil.* Rio de Janeiro: Forense, 2005, v. 14.

Wald, Arnoldo (Org.).. *Direito das coisas.* 11. ed. São Paulo: Saraiva, 2002.

Wald, Arnoldo (Org.).. *Obrigações e contratos.* 16. ed. São Paulo: Saraiva, 2004.

Wieacker, Franz. *História do direito privado moderno.* Trad. de Antônio Manuel Hespanha. 3. ed. Lisboa: Fundação Gulbenkian, 1993.

Zanetti, Ana Carolina. *Contrato de distribuição:* o inadimplemento recíproco. São Paulo: Atlas, 2015.

Zanetti, Cristiano de Souza. *Responsabilidade pela ruptura das negociações.* São Paulo: Editora Juarez de Oliveira, 2005.

Index

The numbers here refer to paragraph numbers.

Absence (legal concept), 281–282
Acceptance, 189–195, 199, 201–202, 204–205, 210–214, 255, 265
Accessory or ancillary duties (related to mutual cooperation and collaboration), 156–157, 456. *See also* Obligation
Act of God, 133. *See also* Liability; Force majeure
Actio pauliana, lat. (action against infringement of legal rights of the creditors), 402–409
Actual transmission of the object, 192
Agency, 505–521
Agency and distribution agreements, 510–521
Arbitration, 368–376, 748
Association, 70, 751, 768
Autonomous trade representative, 508
Avoidance; Nullity, 323–328. *See also* Void

Brazil, country, 1
Brazilian Civil Rights Framework for the Internet, 186
Breach (of contract); non-performance, 97, 222, 410, 460, 464–465, 467. *See also* Performance
Building rental, 533–538
Burden of proof, 133–134, 245–247
Businessman. *See* Entrepreneur
Business management (legal concept), 497, 502–503

Clause (types), 339–376
- arbitration clause, 368–376
- exemption clauses, 351–352, 485–491
- implied clauses, 349
- penalty clause, 353–367

Case Law, 46, 53, 116, 163, 214, 232, 248, 266, 270, 411, 603, 629, 770
Commercial Act, 69, 105–106
Commercial Law, 27, 32, 58, 63–70, 154, 666, 765
Commercial Tenancy Law, 537
Concreteness, 38
Condition, 274–338
- contingent condition, 392
- resolutory condition, 392

Consent, 158, 161, 190, 284–312, 313, 315, 322–338, 568, 598, 653, 767
Consumer, 41, 61, 82–85, 238, 303–304, 376, 487, 506–507, 582–584, 629, 657
Contract
- accessory contracts, 92–94
- adhesion contract, 114–118, 210–214, 351, 384, 629
- aleatory contract, 98–102, 388–390
- bilateral contract, 88, 130, 349, 444–445
- civil contract, 583
- classification of contracts, 86–112
- commercial contract, 105–108
- commercial concession contract, 512
- commutative contract, 98, 101–102, 387, 437, 512, 618
- conditional contracts, 385–393
- contract for the benefit of a third party, 399–409
- contracts of delayed performance, 96
- contract, requirements of form, 90–91
- contracts of instantaneous performance, 96
- contracts with the government and public administration, 716–748
- fiduciary contracts, 146
- formal contract, 90–91, 193, 234, 602
- informal contract, 90–91
- multiparty agreement, 194

- not legally standardized or innominate contract, 103
- principal contract, 92–94
- real contract or 'rights *in rem* contracts', 95, 192, 524, 707–708
- redhibitory defect or vice, 102, 573
- standardized or nominate contract, 103
- transfer of contractual rights, 400
- unilateral contract, 87–89, 444, 652, 660, 693, 737

Contractor, 489, 590, 592, 598–602, 605–609, 727, 729, 738, 743
Corporate Law, 765
Corporations, 67, 70, 374, 612, 620, 623
- business corporation, 70
- simple corporations, 70

Creditor, 72, 133, 284, 331, 333, 359, 361, 365, 367, 398, 402, 404, 406–407, 409, 412, 415, 427, 429, 455, 462, 465, 469, 475–477, 560, 590, 647, 651, 655, 660, 668–673, 675–679, 682, 686–687
- secured creditor, 673, 675–679

Culpa in contrahendo, 264–272. *See also* Liability; Pre-contractual liability

Damages, 131, 201, 292, 294–296, 300–301, 337–338, 367, 450, 458, 463–464, 468–471, 485–491, 501, 573, 607, 675, 687, 702
Debtor, 72, 133, 220, 362–364, 367, 404–407, 412, 415–416, 429, 435–436, 454–473, 475, 477, 482, 501, 549, 590, 647, 651, 655, 657–659, 668, 672, 678–679, 682, 684, 701
Death, 22, 280–283, 605, 631, 658–659, 703, 766
- presumptive death, 282
- simultaneous death, 283

Deceit, 285–296, 300, 316, 331, 333
- mutual deceit, 294
- negative deceit, 293
- third-party deceit, 295

Declaration of will, 123, 197, 204, 242
Default, 362, 410, 412–415, 462, 471–473, 573, 677, 715
Defects in consent, 284
Delay in performing a contract obligation, 462
Developer (rel. works contracts), 398, 590, 599, 601–602, 604, 606, 608
Discharge by agreement, 417, 435

Eccessiva onerosità (it.), 436, 439, 443
Employment, 42, 278, 376, 592–595, 598–599. *See also* Works contract
Enterprise, 43, 60, 62, 68–69, 119, 141, 487
Entrepreneur, 67, 507, 754, 756
Error, 265, 285–296, 331, 333, 644
Establishment, 69, 241, 278, 615, 670
Estate Register, 560
Ethical values, 38
Exceptio non adimpleti contractus, 89, 444–445, 453
Exemption clauses, 351–352, 485–491. *See also* Damages

Faulty behaviour of the debtor, 454–473, 605, 631, 741
Force majeure, 133. *See also* Liability; Act of God
Fraud of creditors, 284, 331, 333, 402, 404. *See also Actio pauliana*

Gambling and wagering (contract), 539–552
General conditions of business, 115–116. *See also* Standard-form contracts
Good faith, 25, 81, 143, 147–157, 229, 250, 258, 260, 264, 268–273, 287, 289, 293, 327, 330, 349, 381–383, 393, 422, 426, 430, 457, 466, 501, 546, 700
Goodwill, 69, 536
Gratuitous promises, 216–219

Hardship, 228, 231–232, 412–416. *See also Eccessiva onerosità* (it.)

Impossibility, frustration and hardship: The unforeseen, 412–416
Improper pressure; coercion, 297–301
Internet, 186. *See also* Brazilian Civil Rights Framework for the Internet
Interpretation, 46, 48, 66, 108, 150, 286, 371, 377–384, 430, 645–650, 721
Invalidity (of the contract), 69, 289–291, 299, 323, 325, 408–409, 659. *See also* Nullity; Voidability
Invitation to treat, 198

Joint and several liability. *See* Solidarity
Judiciary, 49–55, 240, 638
Jurisprudence. *See* Case Law

Laesio enormis; usury, 42, 284, 302–309, 312, 322, 331, 333, 535
Land Statute, 534, 537
Landlord, landholder or lessor, 528
Lapse, 480–481
Lease contract, Leasing, 528, 612–613, 616, 628–629, 631
Legal capacity, 42, 83, 135, 276, 568
Legal effectiveness, 211
Legal personality, 274–276, 754, 758
Legal system; legal family, 7–8, 30–46, 72, 76, 78, 85, 104, 146–147, 158, 160, 220, 222, 233, 242, 249, 258, 379, 419, 474, 615
Legal transaction, 91, 191, 241–242, 252–257, 261, 273, 284–285, 289, 292, 294, 296–300, 313–314, 316, 327–328, 331, 333, 337, 393, 578, 612, 667
Lessee, tenant or leaseholder, 528
Liability, 25, 73, 123–124, 126–130, 132–135, 137–143, 246, 248–273, 333, 488, 491, 544, 573, 606–608, 697, 767
  contractual liability and extra-contractual liability. *See* Liability
  joint and several liability. *See* Solidarity
  liability for the solidity of the construction, 606–608
  obligational liability, 123
  pre-contractual liability, 73. *See also Culpa in contrahendo*
Limitation of actions, 474–484. *See also* Statute of limitations
Loan, 688–715
Loan for use, 693–703
Loan for consumption, 704–715

Main obligation, 122, 124, 156–157, 325, 355–356, 359–360, 655. *See also* Obligation
Mandate, 22, 503, 597

Natural obligations, 220, 539, 543
Nebenpflichten (German Doctrine), 157, 456
Non-performance. *See* Breach
Norm (drafting), 158–188
  interpretative dispositive norm, 159
  narrative norms, 165
  perfect, imperfect and more than perfect norms, 164
  suppletive dispositive norm, 159
Notary, 238–244
Nullity, 282, 309, 323–337, 435, 546, 643. *See also* Validity
  absolute nullity, 309, 323–324, 328, 330
  relative nullity or possibility of annulment of the transaction, 324, 331–336

Object, 192, 217, 265, 288, 313–321, 327, 345, 409, 435, 523–524, 530, 560, 565–566, 573, 591, 605, 612, 622, 631, 644, 672–673, 675, 681, 683, 694, 706, 713–714, 732, 756
Obligation, 13, 36, 40, 42, 58, 67, 69, 80–81, 87–89, 99, 102, 108, 122–125, 127–128, 130, 133, 135, 156–157, 164, 180, 201, 216, 220, 245–247, 249, 259–260, 267, 292, 304, 306–307, 310, 325, 349, 352–353, 355–356, 359–360, 362–363, 367, 387–388, 395, 398, 400–401, 418, 431, 433, 435–436, 439, 444–445. 447–449, 451, 456–459, 461–465, 471, 485, 487–488, 491, 499, 513, 519, 523, 531–532, 539, 543–544, 546, 557, 560, 574–578, 632, 635, 640, 647–649, 651–652, 655, 658–659, 660, 666–667, 675–677, 679, 685, 693, 709, 713–714, 718, 730, 750, 765
'Obligation as a process'. *See* Good faith
Offer, 189–214
  offeree, 190, 194, 197–200, 202, 207
  offeror, 190, 194, 197–199, 201–202, 204, 206–207
Operativeness, 38
Ordinations of the Portuguese Kings, 7

Pacta sunt servanda (lat.), 221, 226, 228, 418, 762
Partial community of property, 159
Partnership agreements, 749–770
Partnership's assets (capital social), 763
Penalty. *See* Clause: penalty clause
Performance. *See* Breach
  relative non-performance, 461–462
Pledge, penhor, 663–687
Positive breach of contract, 464–465, 467
Privity of contract, 394–409
Property, 24, 38, 58, 95, 145, 159, 297, 319, 321, 398, 522, 524, 535–536, 554–557, 560–561, 566, 570, 577–578, 605, 664, 666–667, 672, 678, 688, 693,

699, 705–707, 712, 738, 752
rural property, 535
urban property, 535

Qualified silence, 205

Raffles, 551
Rebus sic stantibus (lat.), 223, 226, 603, 741
Remedies, 89, 418–631
Rental agreements, 522–538, 702
Restitution, 498–504

Sale of Goods, 118, 553–585
Secondary duties, 156, 457, 466. *See also* Obligation; *Nebenpflichten*
Settlement, 384, 632–650
Settlement types, 637–642
Silence, 202–203, 205, 293, 315–316. *See also* Qualified silence
Sociability, 38
Solidarity (joint and several liability), 180, 333, 453
Specific performance and injunctions, 424–433
Stable union, 24, 79
Standard-contracts, 351–352
Standard-form contracts, 119–122. *See also* General conditions of business
State of danger, 310–312, 331, 333
Statute of limitations, 408, 477
Supplier, 41, 83, 350, 513, 621–622, 624
Sub contract, 401
Suretyship contract, 384, 651, 655–659
Synallagmatic, 87–89, 444

Tenant, 42, 528, 535–536, 538, 694
Tenancy Law, 183, 527, 534, 537
Termination (rel. contract), 231–232, 262, 273, 410–417, 434–443, 454, 459, 464, 577, 605, 631, 679–680, 691, 697, 703–741, 766–767, 769
Third parties and the contract, 396–398

Undue payment, 497–499, 501
Undue profit on account of another person's loss, 493. *See also* Unjust enrichment
Unilateral Act, 216
Unilateral declaration of will, 123
Unjust enrichment, 495, 497, 536. *See also* Undue profit on account of another person's loss
Usury. *See Laesio enormis*

Validity (of the contract). *See* Invalidity
Void. *See* Nullity
Voidability, 644

Works contract, 429, 490, 586–609, 745. *See also* Employment

www.ingramcontent.com/pod-product-compliance
Lightning Source LLC
Chambersburg PA
CBHW071344230926
51846CB00002B/446